THE LONDON CRAFT BEER GUIDE

JONNY GARRETT
AND BRAD EVANS

10 9 8 7 6 5 4 3 2 1

Ebury Press, an imprint of Ebury Publishing, 20 Vauxhall Bridge Road, London, SW1V 2SA

Ebury Press is part of the Penguin Random House group of companies whose addresses can be found at global.penguinrandomhouse.com

Penguin
Random House
UK

Text and photography © The Craft Beer Channel Ltd. 2018
Illustrations © Alex Foster 2018

Jonny Garrett and Brad Evans have asserted their right to be identified as the author of this Work in accordance with the Copyright, Designs and Patents Act 1988

First published by Ebury Press in 2018
www.penguin.co.uk

A CIP catalogue record for this book is available from the British Library

Design: James Pople

ISBN: 9781785035562

Colour reproduction by Altaimage Ltd, London
Printed and bound in China by C&C Offset Printing Co., Ltd

Penguin Random House is committed to a sustainable future for our business, our readers and our planet. This book is made from Forest Stewardship Council® certified paper.

MIX
Paper from
responsible sources
FSC® C018179
www.fsc.org

THE BEST BREWERIES, PUBS AND TAP ROOMS · FOR THE BEST ARTISAN BREWS ·

THE
LONDON
CRAFT BEER
GUIDE

JONNY GARRETT AND BRAD EVANS

EBURY
PRESS

CONTENTS

INTRODUCTION: BEER HERE NOW

6

NORTH

10

SOUTH

76

EAST
130

WEST
182

CENTRAL
224

CHOOSING A LONDON PUB
252

BEER HERE NOW
CRAFT BEER IN THE CAPITAL

**IT HASN'T ALWAYS BEEN THIS GOOD. A DECADE AGO,
BREWING IN THE CAPITAL WAS NEARLY EXTINCT.**

———

Back then there were just 10 breweries, and many of those wouldn't live to see the craft beer revolution take off. Since reaching its peak of 115 breweries in 1830, this world-famous trading hub had let one of its most famous exports go down the drain. The dockworkers had abandoned their porters, and pale ale breweries were being bought out and closed all over the city. Names like Charringtons and Taylor Walker were consigned to history, just words etched in stone above pubs, while the buildings were left derelict, the tall chimneys blocked up and coppers reclaimed.

By the 1970s most bars' cellars were full of the dull, mass-produced lagers that had helped ruin real ale, championed by suited men who knew nothing about beer but plenty about profit. As they cashed in, the pubs went into decline, drowning under rising rents and thinning margins. Forced to drink overpriced pseudo-brews, drinkers were forgetting how beer was supposed to taste.

The Campaign for Real Ale (CAMRA) hadn't given up though. In 1971, over a few drinks in Dunquin, Ireland, four men swore to fight for the survival of traditional cask beer. For the next 30 years they battled to keep real ale alive, running festivals, publishing pamphlets and hounding the government. It became one of the biggest consumer movements in the world, but the British pub and its traditional beers were still in danger. First resigned to bad lager, then bored by it, drinking tins at home became the norm as supermarkets discounted their beer to irresponsible levels in the hope of attracting shoppers. The greatest brewing nation on Earth had become homogenous, bloated and boring.

Thankfully, a nation famous for its complete lack of brewing heritage was bored too, and a revolution had just begun that would change everything. New varieties of aromatic hops, originally developed to be more disease resistant, were falling into the hands of homebrewers in California, Oregon and Washington. Most of these beer nerds were brewing British bitters and historic IPA recipes, but the experimental hops were adding extra dimensions to the beer – they were much more bitter, but the trade-off was hints of pine, resin and grapefruit unheard of in beer before. Excited by what they had discovered, many of these brewers decided to go pro – people like Ken Grossman of Sierra Nevada Brewing Company. This movement spawned the American pale ale and IPA, two styles that changed the way the world looked at beer.

But while new-fangled 'craft' beer spread across the USA in the 80s and 90s, in the UK things were still looking bleak. Tens of pubs were closing across the country every week. Continental lagers were able to market themselves as premium, ripping out real ale lines and the heart of British tradition. Pockets of local, traditional breweries survived in the Black Country and Yorkshire, but in London we celebrated the Millennium with Prosecco and discount cans of Carling. To many it was the darkest hour in the history of British beer.

In a lock-up opposite Charlton Athletic's stadium a man called Alastair Hook was taking a different view. He'd studied brewing at Heriot-Watt University before heading to Bavaria, where he did an apprenticeship at the oldest brewery in the world, Weihenstephan. As a pupil of German brewing he was never going to be the saviour of real ale, but he did have ambitions to change British beer. To start, he focused on traditional German styles like Helles and Weissbier and back then that was pretty revolutionary – the idea of a London lager was certainly brave. It didn't take him long to outgrow the garage and move to Greenwich, where he assumed the name Meantime, after the longitude that dissects that part of town. Meantime showed that artisan beer had a place in the UK, but over the next decade only a few new breweries joined the ranks in London while others closed or moved.

It was actually a tiny town near Aberdeen where America's revolution truly hit our shores. Fraserburgh is just about the least likely place in the world for a modern US-inspired brewery to spring up, but the one that did went on to kick open doors all over the UK. Brash and controversial, BrewDog were exactly the kind of company needed to challenge the powerful corporations that owned the market. Their beer was hoppy as hell, high in alcohol and branded, it seemed, to cause offence.

Faced with vocal opposition, the founders Martin Dickie and James Watt were unapologetic, locking horns with anyone who tried to moderate them. Whatever you think of their marketing approach, their beers are regularly cited as an influence by some of the UK's greatest brewers. One such brewer is Evin O'Riordain of The Kernel, who stands at head of the London craft brewery family tree. Unlike BrewDog though, Evin had no ambitions beyond the walls of his brewery. He simply wanted to brew big-flavoured American craft beer. As it turns out, that was a solid business strategy.

It wasn't just Evin's exciting beers or successful business that encouraged others: it was how he went about creating them. He believed in experimentation: he never brewed the same beer twice and rejected all advertising and marketing. He broke every rule in the start-up book, but the business model he cobbled together has been copied by brewers all over the country. Since he opened The Kernel in 2010, the number of breweries in London has grown from 10 to 100 – a rate of more than one every month. By 2019 there will be more breweries than there have been at any time in the capital's history.

This book tells the tale of this remarkable revolution. It doesn't take the form of a history book or novel; it has no beginning and certainly no ending. It's a collection of short stories about fleeting moments, magical places and incredible people, all of which have come together to create something envied the world over. This is a snapshot of what it is like to live and drink in London today.

What follows isn't just the tap lists and opening times of the best bars or breweries in London, it's an account of the people and places that come together to form a counterculture.

Some people think that craft beer is a bubble, set to burst when something new and exciting comes along. But what you'll find in this book are stories that will be told in a hundred years, backed up by bricks and mortar that have reinvigorated parts of the capital.

Split geographically, we've covered every inch of London in search of the places that tell the story of its brewing's rebirth. The result is a love letter to beer and its place in the greatest city in the world.

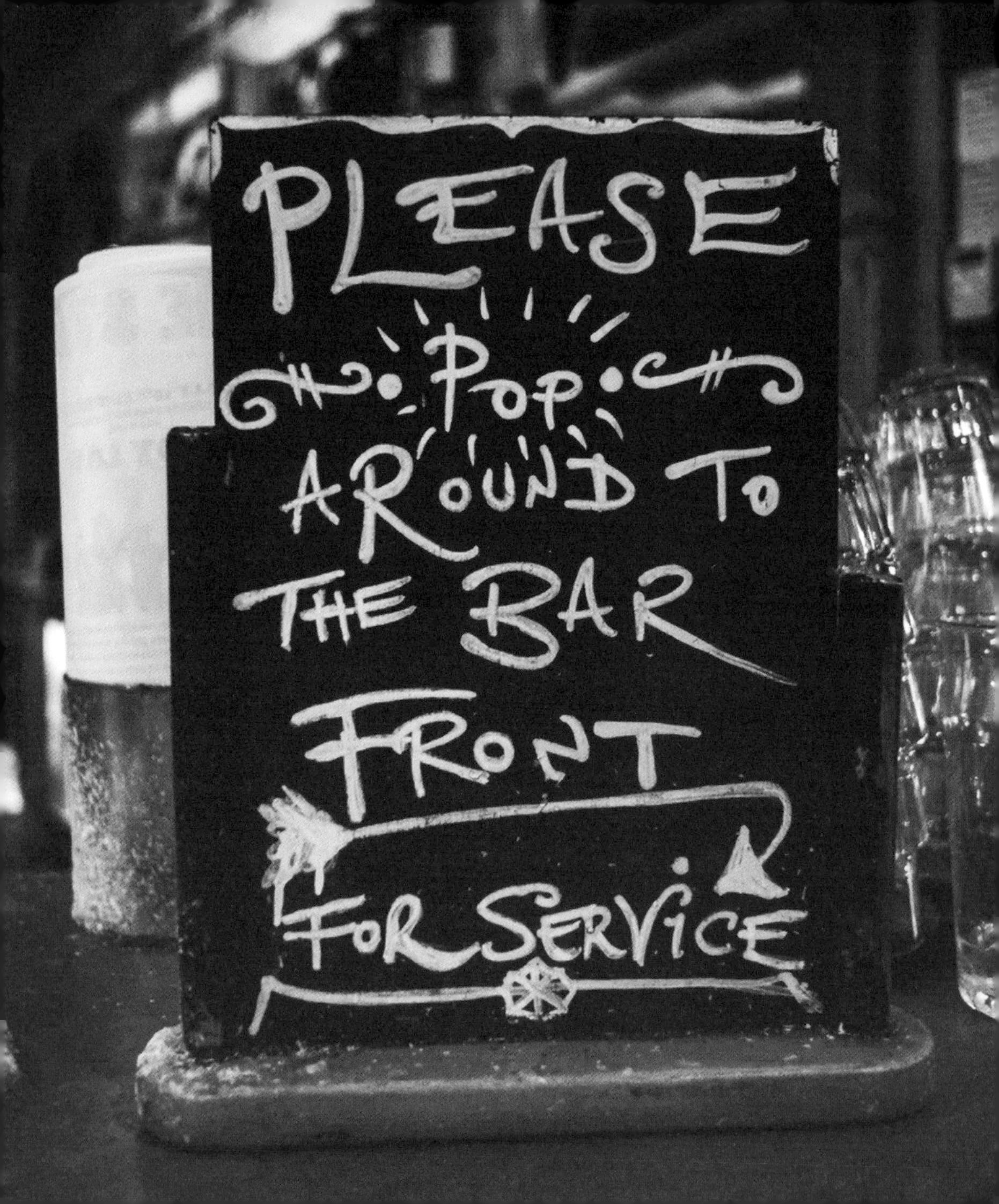
PLEASE
POP
AROUND TO
THE BAR
FRONT
FOR SERVICE

NORTH

LONDON

GETTING OUT OF THE NORTH END OF CAMDEN IS LIKE SURFACING
FROM UNDERWATER. YOU'VE MADE IT THROUGH THE TOURIST STREETS
WHERE NO ONE KNOWS IF THEY ARE PEDESTRIANISED OR JUST
TOO CROWDED, TO A MAGICAL PLACE WHERE RED BUSES REACH
THEIR FINAL STOP AND HIGH RISES DON'T BLOCK OUT THE SUN.

In some directions it feels like you've gone back in time. Take a trip through Dickensian Primrose Hill and pop into the Princess, or through Highgate Cemetery to the Bull, or across the Heath to the Spaniards Inn. Many of the pubs up here feel different; more like a village pub than a capital's. Walking in you half expect the bar staff to know your name. I've had more conversations with strangers stood at the bar in the Southampton Arms than I have collectively throughout the capital.

The charm of these parts of north London is that they don't feel like London at all. You can stand in the middle of Hampstead Heath and not even see the city. Yet all the breweries and pubs in this chapter are still in zone two, not twenty minutes' journey from Euston Station. One, in fact, isn't even twenty seconds away.

The amount of good pubs north of the Euston Road is epic, and while it's not the most concentrated area for breweries in London, it is home to two of the most important. The story of the biggest, Camden Town Brewery, is remarkable. Aside from Meantime it is by far the biggest to have come out of the capital's revolution and is still the only one focused on craft lager. Of course, whether it is still craft after its sale to AB InBev is down to your point of view, but it proved to the world that craft brewing is a legitimate business rather than a bubble set to burst.

Beavertown have achieved the same but in a very different way. Now on their third site and still growing faster than anyone thought possible, they have become an inspiration for hundreds of independent UK breweries by constantly breaking the rules. Not only are their beers big, hoppy monsters, but they were one of the first breweries to go into can, didn't brew a core IPA for over four years, and have created a brand so far removed from traditional tropes that most people wouldn't know they were a brewery. Their presence in desperately uncool Tottenham Hale has helped revitalise the area and form a small, creative hub in a former industrial wasteland – a wasteland that now gets thousands of drinkers visiting it every weekend.

THE DUKE'S HEAD

THE STAG

THE SOUTHAMPTON ARMS

THE ROSE & CROWN

KRIS WINES

CAMDEN TOWN BREWERY

CAPS AND TAPS

HAMMERTON BREWERY

EUSTON TAP

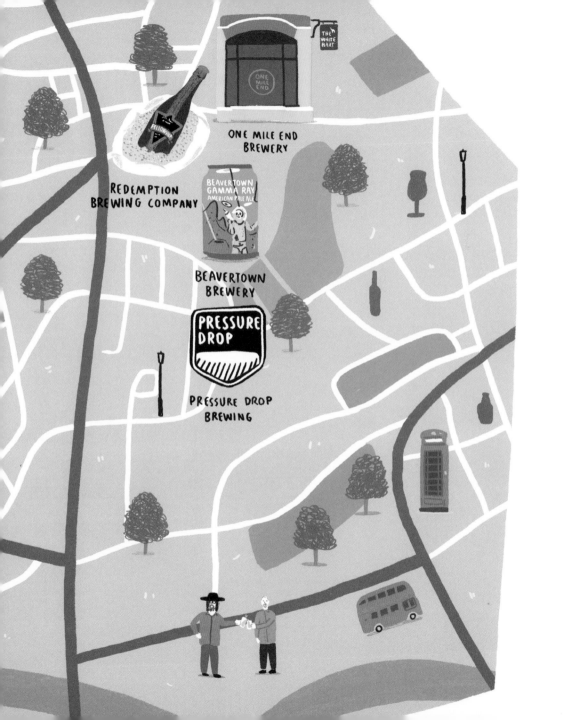

ONE MILE END
BREWERY

REDEMPTION
BREWING COMPANY

BEAVERTOWN
GAMMA RAY
AMERICAN PALE ALE

BEAVERTOWN
BREWERY

PRESSURE
DROP

PRESSURE DROP
BREWING

THE
WHITE
HART

THE SOUTHAMPTON ARMS

THESOUTHAMPTONARMS.CO.UK

THE REAL ALE PUMPS, CASH-ONLY TILL AND RECORD PLAYER MAKE CROSSING THE THRESHOLD OF THIS PUB FEEL LIKE STEPPING BACK IN TIME – AND THE AMOUNT OF TIME YOU LOSE IN THERE CAN STACK UP PRETTY QUICKLY.

You don't realise how perfect the Southampton Arms is until you walk into a different pub. Once you have been to this truly wholesome place, every other pub you drink in will be a disappointment in some way. Despite opening in 2009, The Southampton Arms seems ancient. Perhaps it's the sepia-toned portraits on the walls, or uneven wooden floor, rickety stools and chipped paint. Perhaps it's that you can't pay by card and the food menu is childishly scrawled on a tiny blackboard.

Or maybe it's that, with the exception of two taps, all the beers and ciders are on cask. For all its charms, this is what makes The Southampton Arms unique. Ten pumps of cask ales and six real ciders stretch along the bar, and – unlike in just about every other London pub – you know each one is going to be in perfect condition. Ash the landlord knows how to pick great beers, but even more, he knows how to cellar them. After seven years of looking after the trickiest form of pub booze, he knows exactly how every style should taste and when to get them on the bar. Don't underestimate how hard that is to achieve.

'It takes a lot of work, a lot of care and attention and a lot of running up and down stairs checking them', he says. 'We turn over a lot here so you have to create new, inventive ways of making sure they are on form at the right time. We started with eight pumps, which was a pretty risky start. Nobody knew if it would work, especially being a little community pub like this. But within a week or two we knew we needed more.'

Put simply, real ale or cask beer is sent out to the pub before it's ready – it's put in barrels and shipped while still unconditioned. The benefit is that it means the publican can start serving the second it's ready – and fresh beer is the best beer. But it also means the brewer is putting a lot of faith in the publican to look after the liquid and serve it at the right time. Sadly most don't, so you should always ask for a taster before buying a real ale. But in The Southampton I don't bother. From Redemption's

NORTH LONDON • The Southampton Arms

Big Chief brewed just a few miles away to Magic Rock's seminal High Wire made up in Huddersfield, I know the beer is going to be good – and even better with a homemade pork pie or crusty roast bap.

Flavour aside, there are loads of other reasons to visit The Southampton Arms. They run what has to be the hardest pub quiz in London – one in which we honestly celebrated getting half marks. It's hosted by a man usually drunk by the end of the first question and hoarse by the second. If the quizmaster isn't mouthing off (on one memorable night calling one drinker a c*** for revealing an answer), you might be able to hear the selection of old-school jazz, blues and rock records kept in a dusty corner behind the bar. On other nights you'll get one of the locals on the piano, giving the pub a Western saloon feel.

In any other bar these events might feel cynically hipster. But completely devoid of hype, pomp and fashion this pub manages to do achingly hip things while making it all completely natural. From the perfectly balanced but unpretentious beer list to the humble attempts to keep drinkers entertained, it's like the whole place was designed for the benefit of the quiet, cask-loving publican. It just so happens we all love his way of doing things.

I have never felt more instantly at home than at this pub. It is the embodiment of everything that is brilliant about beer, and my number one pub in the world.

BEERS	TEN CASK, SIX CIDERS, TWO KEG.	
CULTURE	BY DAY IT'S ALL CROSSWORDS AND QUIET PINTS, BY NIGHT A ROWDY SATURDAY NIGHT IN A COUNTRY PUB. GET THERE EARLY.	

NORTH LONDON • The Southampton Arms

THE DUKE'S HEAD

THEDUKESHEADHIGHGATE.CO.UK

LOOKING DOWN ON LONDON FROM THE TOP OF HIGHGATE, THE DUKE'S HEAD FEELS A WORLD AWAY FROM THE HUSTLE OF THE CITY, COMBINING A VILLAGE PUB FEEL WITH THE BEST INDEPENDENT BRITISH BEER, CIDER AND GIN.

London has over eight million people living in it. It stretches 20 miles from the Thames Estuary, unbroken until it nearly swallows Slough. But our capital isn't some giant complex of grey concrete from east to west. It has grown in fits and starts, leaving gaps, green lands and missing connections. Really it is a collection of neighbourhoods all completely distinct from each other.

The great London drinking holes feel like village pubs – and it's because they are. They absorb all that is vital about an area to create a space that reflects it, and here Highgate is embodied in its softly spoken, almost Church of England-like calm. Well, some of the time.

Found near the top of the hill that looms over Archway Station, it is in a wealthy but understated part of north London. With Victorian shop fronts, leafy cemeteries and detached housing, the only clue you're in London is the red buses that roll down the hill towards the City. Otherwise the high street could be anywhere in the Home Counties.

The pub itself has huge single-glazed windows perfect for people-watching, but also for warming up

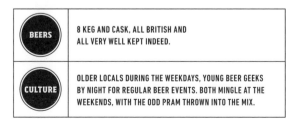

BEERS	8 KEG AND CASK, ALL BRITISH AND ALL VERY WELL KEPT INDEED.
CULTURE	OLDER LOCALS DURING THE WEEKDAYS, YOUNG BEER GEEKS BY NIGHT FOR REGULAR BEER EVENTS. BOTH MINGLE AT THE WEEKENDS, WITH THE ODD PRAM THROWN INTO THE MIX.

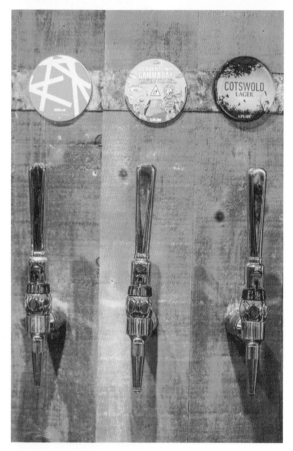

your pint. That's OK though, because the focus in The Duke's Head is on traditional cask ale, so it's meant to be a more ambient temperature anyway. The owners take great pride in their cellar and with eight carefully chosen, all-British handpulls you're guaranteed a good pint whenever you go in. Drinking fresh is vital when it comes to living cask beer. If you're not sure what to have, look at the man at the end of the counter because he's probably asked the right questions. It's the kind of place where the locals all sit at the bar and drink their way through a cask of their favourite then somehow walk away sober as a judge.

If the pumps aren't exciting you there are eight keg lines too, shooting out of a column in the middle of the back bar. You might think that keeping to purely British beers would mean a lot of repetition, but such is the strength of British brewing these days that the daily lists are fascinating, thirst-inducing pieces of literature. Their website is constantly updated with what's live and what's waiting in the cellar, so you can make sure it's up to scratch before you make the trip.

You'll always find something delicious from Burning Sky, BrewDog or Cloudwater but local beers seem to be the main order of the day, with Londoners Five Points and Hammerton almost always on tap. If things get really serious, the regional boozing doesn't have to stop there – the pub is also home to the Sacred Gin bar, a cocktail menu made exclusively with gin from the Sacred distillery in Highgate.

While some pubs can make non-regulars feel a little out of place, everyone is a local at The Duke's Head from the moment they walk through the door. Rather than just benefitting the community, it has become one. On the wall opposite the bar is a wooden plaque bearing the names of those who have done the pub great service – usually in the form of spending all their money there. In return for swearing on the horns of a stag that also adorns the walls, the lucky few are given the freedom of the Duke's Head. I doubt that means they can wander into the kitchens or pour themselves a pint, but it certainly makes you feel special every time you walk in. That said, we're still waiting for our invite.

CASK

BERKSHIRE
Sussex
NORTH YORKSHIRE
HACKNEY

ISLINGTON
BERKSHIRE
Bristol
HEREFORDSHIRE
SUSSEX

UP NEXT...

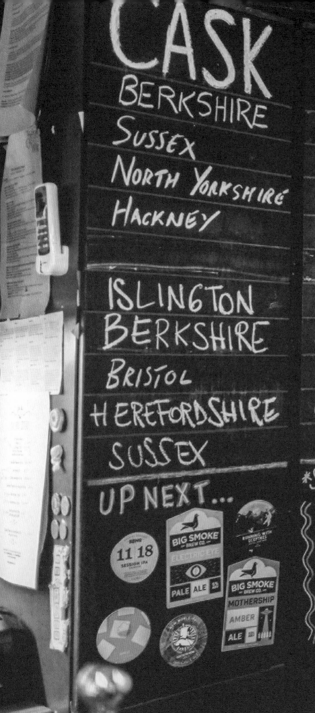

OTT'S BEER

SIREN - PROTEUS VOL...
GUN BREWERY - SCARAMANGA...
BAD CO. - LOVE OVER GOL...
FIVE POINTS - DERAILED

HAMMERTON - N7 -
SIREN - UNDERCURR...
Bristol Beer Factory - Twelve...
OLIVER'S - MEDIUM
SEACIDER - HARDCORE...

* STAFF ARE DRINKING ... *

CHARLIE → TIDAL WAVE
MARS → FRETTIN PEAT
BEARD → AFF IT ... FOR NOW!
LILY → DABINETT
JONNY → IRN BRU
         SEACIDER
SARAHLEE → LEMONADE MATE
AISHA → NOR'HOP
SASKIA → GAMMA RAY
GEORGIE →
OSCAR → ...ber City

EUSTON TAP

EUSTONTAP.COM

A LONDONER COMMUTER INSTITUTION, THE EUSTON TAP
HAS CAUSED MORE MISSED CONNECTIONS THAN SOUTHERN
TRAINS THANKS TO THE 47 WELL-CURATED BEERS ON TAP.

As I place my pint on the rickety metal table, it nearly tips. I snatch my drink from the brink and clutch it to my chest instead. The Euston Tap is not really designed for drinking in. Originally the squat gatehouse that formed part of the arch outside Euston Station, the owners have done little to make it more comfortable for punters. The bar staff have more room than the drinkers, the spiral staircase is tight enough to tie you in knots, and anyone over six foot has to stoop where the few tables are. It's fair to say they have packed it all in though; over 40 taps of great beer and two fridges keep people coming back, and can sometimes leave the queue trailing out the door as people struggle to make their choice. Inside gets cramped so I'm stood leaning against the railing opposite the entrance. In this exposed position you have to be wary of wing mirrors as the buses come close around the corner but it's the best place to watch the daily phenomenon that happens on this pub's doorstep. Come five o'clock it's like a scene from a David Attenborough documentary, as the entire north London commuter belt migrates through Euston Station. You can almost hear Sir David's voiceover as a herd of suits head around the corner, checking watches and calculating: time for a swifty?

What I love about the Euston Tap is it so easily could have been a bad train-station boozer. It could have served macro lagers and bad snacks to commuters happy to drink whatever was put in front of them. Instead, it has been serving some of the best beer in London since before most craft beer drinkers had

BEERS	OVER THIRTY-ONE KEG AND SIXTEEN CASK ACROSS THE TWO SITES, 150 BOTTLES/CANS – THAT MIGHT JUST BE A RECORD IN LONDON!
CULTURE	THIS IS AN EVENING AND WINTER PUB. POP BY AFTER RUSH HOUR FOR A BUSTLING, EXCITABLE FEEL WITH A GOOD MIX OF SUITS, BEER NERDS AND PLEASANTLY SURPRISED TOURISTS.

NORTH LONDON • Euston Tap

earned beards. The American-branded tap handles behind the bar are a testament to the brews they've had on tap, but they rarely correspond to what is actually pouring. Instead you have to look up at the blackboards above to see what's available. The US and the UK are always best represented – the owners evidently love IPAs as much as the rest of the world – but the selection is well curated.

I've spent many happy hours drinking Lagunitas IPA and dodging rain showers at my favourite railing, as well as several steamy winter evenings in the crowded upstairs, ploughing through the cask pumps. With the huge turnover of beer here you are almost guaranteed to have a fresh pint, which is very important for the hoppy beers they prefer to serve.

Until recently the Euston Tap also ran the Cider Tap across the road, which was a mirror image of the original site except that it served real cider. In early 2017 this was given a refurb to become the East Lodge, a classier second wing of the Euston Tap pouring different beers in a brighter, less chaotic atmosphere. It lacks some of the atmosphere of its grimier brother but it's novel to drink in sunlight for a change.

Given the number of people who have popped in for a pint with no clue about beer and walked away with a revelatory pint in their hands, no London pub has converted more beer lovers than the Euston Tap.

NORTH LONDON • Euston Tap

REAL ALE

REAL ALE IS A TERM THAT A BUNCH OF 70'S BEER NERDS CAME UP WITH TO DEFINE AND PROTECT TRADITIONAL CASK BEER.

———

Already rare elsewhere in the world, they hoped to save real ale from extinction. CAMRA, as they are more commonly known, defined it as beer brewed from traditional ingredients, matured by secondary fermentation in the container from which it is dispensed, and served without any extraneous gas. In layman's terms, it's beer that conditions in the pub cellar until it tastes perfect, at which point it's handpumped up and into the glass. The idea is it is as fresh as can be when it hits your lips, and at a temperature where you can taste all the subtleties.

Against all the odds, by which I mean the huge marketing budgets of these global brewers, they succeeded in keeping cask alive. Real ale is now an almost uniquely British phenomenon that, thanks to the craft revolution, is growing once again. Good cask beer tastes fresh in a way that is hard to explain. It is moreish, alive with flavour and vibrant on your tongue. It's both refreshing and hearty at the same time – the fruit, bread, citrus and bitterness all come together in perfect harmony in a way few kegged beers can replicate.

But cask beer suffers from two major flaws. The first is that it doesn't really suit hoppy or strong beers, the two keystones of modern brewing. Without carbonation the beers can get sticky and residually bitter, so many great beers wouldn't work so well on cask. More importantly, a lot of cask beer is very bad indeed. It's

not the brewers' fault though. Looking after cask beer takes training. You need to care for your cellar, manage your beers so they don't sit around too long, and know exactly when to tap them. Sadly, a huge percentage served in London hasn't had this care and attention, going flat and tasting of either cardboard or vinegar. The most important thing to do when considering a cask beer in a pub is to ask for a taster.

There are, however, plenty of London pubs that know exactly how to look after cask beer. Some even focus on it, like the fantastic Southampton Arms, Cock Tavern and Wenlock Arms. I can't recall ever having a bad pint in any of these places and they take great pride in how they serve their beers. The Harp and the Old Fountain are also bastions of good cask beer in central London and The Duke's Head in Highgate has a well-kept range too.

There are a few tell-tale signs when looking for good real ale. Turnover has to be fast, so places with a few handpumps implies they have a lot of real ale drinkers to keep turnover high – if it's just one or two pumps, it's not their focus. Some pubs put up signs of what is coming on tap soon or list it on the pub's website, which shows a well-managed cellar, which is key.

A little knowledge goes a long way in making sure you only ever drink good beer. In the case of cask, it's the difference between a revelatory pint and a swift return to the bar.

THE ROSE & CROWN

ROSEANDCROWNKENTISHTOWN.COM

A NEW TAKE ON THE LOCAL BOOZER, THE ROSE & CROWN
OFFERS FANTASTIC CRAFT BEER AND QUARTERLY KITCHEN
POP-UPS WITH COMEDY NIGHTS AND QUIZZES TO KEEP
LOCALS COMING BACK AGAIN AND AGAIN.

———

In the UK tens of pubs close every week. The sight of boarded-up country inns – which once were symbols and centres of community – is desperately sad. As much as craft beer has done wonders for the industry, for every craft beer place that opens, tens of pubs shut their doors forever. Mostly they become expensive flats or a supermarket, occasionally they're just reduced to rubble. But sometimes the doors close, sealing in the oak, faded carpets and period features like a cocoon that springs open again filled with new life. That's exactly what has happened at The Rose & Crown in Kentish Town.

I first visited the pub when it was called the Torriano back in 2013. The Libertines had played there in their early years, but its cool dive days were behind it. Far from being Shoreditch chic, the exposed brickwork made you doubt the walls' structural integrity and the look of the taps made you think twice about drinking anything that wasn't in a sealed container. The barman dusted off some very old Punk IPA and I sat on a collapsed sofa to question my life choices.

The pub's new owner, Theo Caudell, had been questioning some of his own around that time. Working at a pub and stock auditing company, his job had been to visit pubs regularly, and he'd seen what worked and what didn't. Increasingly he realised it was the beers on offer that mattered most. For somebody so intimately aware of the work that goes on behind the scenes, choosing a place that needed so much work seems strange.

'I'd been here once before back in the day, I remembered it as being a pretty dodgy pub. But the owner was really kind, took us around and within five minutes we were like "we can see this". There was definitely scope there to make something, we saw it as a kind of blank canvas.'

But some blank canvases need more than a lick of paint. Theo and his two partners, Ben Caudell and Chris Hurd, had to strip out the tap lines, completely

NORTH LONDON • The Rose & Crown

gut the garden and probably stick some girders up too. For everything that changed, though, something remained. The gigs still happen downstairs with an emphasis on comedy, there's a devilishly difficult pub quiz every Tuesday, and the central bar is a huge part of the pub's identity.

The biggest difference is the beer. The central column holding the whole ceiling up is covered with beer mats from breweries all over the world. Some of the most experimental names in the craft beer industry are on there. In particular War Pigs, Cloudwater and Verdant sit next to the safer options of Brooklyn and Fourpure, who offer delicious lagers and lighter styles for those overwhelmed by the main four-out font.

Spread across the bar you'll find small clipboards with the kitchen menu on them. The food here is as unpredictable as the beer because the kitchen staff change four times a year, with pop-up chefs giving way to each other to offer the regulars something new. We've had dirty, delicious barbecue food, refined Italian aperitivo and some of the best tapas we've ever tasted over the last year – a far cry from what came before, which was probably a Breville out back.

Such a huge change can't have been easy for the locals to get used to. The pub has been completely reinvented and occasionally tainted with the same paint-by-numbers brush many people use for craft beer bars – hipster, elitest, calculated. But for me there aren't many more welcoming bars in the whole of London.

'So we're two years in. The first six months were difficult. It was that transformation period and older locals were coming in and saying "six pounds a pint? You havin' a laugh!" and we bit our lip.'

Now they don't have to.

BEERS	SIX KEG, TWO CASK. FOURPURE AND BROOKLYN ON CONSTANTLY, BUT BESIDES THAT, WHO KNOWS?
CULTURE	RELAXED AND YOUNG. EXPECT DJS LATER ON WEEKENDS BUT A LOCAL BOOZER VIBE THE REST OF THE WEEK.

THE STAG

PUB

THESTAGNW3.COM

**ONE OF THE BEST PUB GARDENS IN LONDON MAKES THIS
AN UNBEATABLE PLACE TO SPEND A SUMMER EVENING,
BUT COME WINTER THE HUGE BEER SELECTION AND GREAT
FOOD MEANS IT'S A BRILLIANT COSY HAUNT TOO.**

Your eureka beer is the pint that changes the way you drink forever. It's the beer that you hold up to the light, bemused at how any drink could be so surprising, so unique, so delicious. From that moment on you are 'into beer', and no mass-produced lager or stale bitter is ever going to cut it again.

I had that pint in The Stag in Hampstead. Caught off-guard by the huge selection of draught and bottled beer, I did what you should never do: I judged a book by its cover and went for the showiest. This beer was Red Hook Longhammer, the tap handle of which is a foot-long sledgehammer. Hefty enough to knock a real nail in, when the barman poured it the hammer arched down and bounced satisfyingly.

But it wasn't half as satisfying as the beer. It was the first true American IPA I had ever had and it was like nothing I had tasted before. Caramel, grapefruit and lemon all popped on my tongue as the heady aromas hit the back of my skull, exciting synapses I didn't even know I had. It was revelatory, like riding a bike for the first time. It opened up all kinds of opportunities. From then on, instead of walking into a bar and looking at the taps for something

BEERS	SIXTEEN KEG, FOUR CASK, COUNTLESS IN THE FRIDGES.
CULTURE	BY DAY HAMPSTEAD CHIC, BY NIGHT YOUNG, HIP AND FRIENDLY.

I knew I started looking for something I didn't know. Every pub visit became the chance for a new experience.

Back then in 2011 finding great craft beer wasn't easy. Most of the bars and even breweries in this book opened a while after that. So to have The Stag as my local was a godsend. This massive corner building, painted an imposing charcoal black and decked in oak from floor to ceiling, has become like a second home to me. In winter it's a cosy L-shaped bar with small tables, a wood fire and delicious hearty food. But on a balmy summer night it is my favourite place to be in London. It has one of the best beer gardens in the capital, with big sharing tables, a BBQ constantly on the go and a canned beer fridge so you don't even have to go into the shade to get a round in. On summer Sundays they host acoustic nights, so you can ignore the impending Monday for just a little longer as the soft music and beer soothes you.

The beer list is something special too. Ignore the macro beers they still seem to feel they need and you'll find an eclectic selection of American, British and German beers on tap with tens of beers from all around the world in the fridges too. They are all on rotation so put a week between visits and you'll have a completely new range to choose from.

With great beer and food this pub gets busy at peak times. The upside to this is that it attracts some pretty distinguished guests. On one memorable occasion I sat on the table next to Mel C. If The Stag is good enough for Sporty Spice, it's probably good enough for you.

A LITTLE BIT

WHATS
GOING
ON ??
⟶

BEER	BREWER	STYLE	ABV	P HA
GUINNESS	GUINNESS	STOUT	4.1%	2.3
APA	TAPIT (SA)	APA	6%	3.8
GOLD	CORNISH ORCHARD	CIDER	4.5%	2.4
FRONTIER	FULLERS	LAGER	4.5%	2.50
SESSION IPA	ISLAND RECORDS	SIPA	4.5%	3.2
TAP 1	SCHNEIDER	WHEAT	5.2%	3.2
LEMMY AV'IT	FIERCE	SOUR	5%	3.4
HELLS	CAMDEN	LAGER	4.6%	2.50
ELDERFLOWER	THISTLY CROSS	CIDER	4.0%	3.25
PINK GRAPEFRUIT IPA	KEES (H)	IPA	6%	4
BOLTMAKER	TIM TAYLORS	BITTER	4.1%	2.3
ORKNEY IPA	SWANNAY	IPA	4.8%	2.4

BEER HEAVEN

*= SOLD IN ½ + 2/3 PINTS *

BEER	BREWER	STYLE	ABV	PRICE Half	PRICE Pint
4-GRAINS	TWICKENHAM	PALE	4.5	2.1	4.2
PALE No.1	HOWLING HOPS	PALE	3.8%	2.10	4.20
IPA CITRA	KERNEL	IPA	6.7%	4.0	8.0
VIER	BECKS	LAGER	4%	2.4	4.5
HELLS	CAMDEN	LAGER	4.6%	2.5	5
PRIDE + JOY	VOCATION	APA	5.3%	3	6
REPARATIONS BAJER	TO ØL	G.F. PALE	5.8%	4.40	5.80 2/3RDS
NECK OIL	BEAVERTOWN	SESSION IPA	4.3%	2.60	5.20
UNDERCURRENT	SIREN	OAT PALE	4.5%	2.8	5.30
TOKYO GREEN	THREE BOYS NZ	GREEN TEA PALE ALE	4.5%	4.00	530 2/3RDS
PALE ALE	SIERRA NEVADA	APA	50%	3.30	6.50
03/05	BBNO	U.S. PORTER	6.1%	3.20	6.40

SPECIAL

DRAUGHT

CRAFTY BEER BOOZE *

BEAVERTOWN

BEAVERTOWNBREWERY.CO.UK

WHAT STARTED AS A PASSION PROJECT IN THE BASEMENT OF A
HACKNEY BARBECUE JOINT HAS BECOME ONE OF THE GREAT
CRAFT BEER SUCCESS STORIES – MOSTLY THANKS TO GAMMA RAY,
AN AMERICAN PALE ALE MOST USA BREWERIES ARE ENVIOUS OF.

There's a crass term for famous brewery owners like Logan Plant, one that shows how far the cult of craft beer has come: the 'rockstar brewer'. These are people who make making beer so cool they become celebrities themselves. Most brewers rubbish the idea – there's no way to romanticise the early starts and endless cleaning – but with Logan it fits.

When he decided to open a brewery, he was in the middle of a US tour with his band Sons of Albion. He'd been on the cusp of stardom for many years and never broken through. Tired of being away from his young family, home was calling to him and he was looking for a way out. After a gig he and his drummer headed to Brooklyn's awesome Fette Sau, a converted garage barbecue joint famed for its brisket and beer range.

'Walking in was a real head-slap, eureka moment, you know?' he says, smiling. 'It was the smell; the environment. The big jugs of beer and all the taps on the wall … I'd never seen anything like it. I'd found my calling. I literally made my decision to quit there and then, with my drummer still next to me.'

A week later he came back to the UK, cut off his long hair and beard (not knowing it would become the brewer's uniform) and started afresh. He spent £300 on a homebrew kit and started reading every blog, forum and book he could find to learn the core skills needed to open an American-inspired brewpub.

Duke's Brew & Que opened in Hackney in 2012 making the kind of dirty, delicious barbecue he'd fallen for in Brooklyn. He moved his homebrew operation into the cellar and started brewing beers to match the beef and pork ribs – a smoked porter (now called Smog Rocket) and a rye IPA (8 Ball). It wasn't all American-inspired though. Logan is from the Black Country, a part of the UK associated with some of the best bitters ever made. He still loved Bathams Best Bitter, which reminded him of drinking in pubs with his dad back home, so many of his first brews were attempts to

44

FOUNDED

2012.

ORIGINS

IN THE BASEMENT OF LOGAN'S BARBECUE RESTAURANT IN DE BEAUVOIR TOWN, HACKNEY. THE FIRST BEERS WERE 8 BALL AND SMOG ROCKET, DESIGNED TO GO WITH THE PORK RIBS AND BEEF BRISKET SERVED UPSTAIRS.

FLAGSHIP BEER

THIS HAS TO BE GAMMA RAY, THEIR AMERICAN PALE ALE. IT WAS THE BEER THAT PUT DUKE'S ON THE MAP, WITH ITS LIGHT BISCUIT BODY AND UMBONGO-LIKE AROMA. AT 5.4% IT DRINKS LIGHTER THAN IT HAS ANY RIGHT TO, FIZZING OFF THE TONGUE WITH LOTS OF CITRIC FLAVOURS AND RASPING BITTERNESS.

recreate it. In fact, Beavertown's session IPA, Neck Oil, started life as that recipe. It is now a very different beast, but the drinkability of the best bitter is something you see in all of Beavertown's core beers.

The brewpub concept, which was almost unheard of in modern London, got Logan plenty of attention, but it wasn't until he brewed his first pale ale six months in that heads really started turning. At the time it was probably the best beer being made in London and it wasn't just the taste getting people excited.

'With Gamma Ray we'd hit this kind of tropical, juicy thing. Then Nick [Dwyer, now creative director], who was a waiter in Duke's at the time but also drawing some of our labels, drew a spacemen design. We sold a little bit to a bar down the road and the owner said "Everyone was ordering the spaceman beer! They didn't even care what it was." And I was like, "Fuck, we're marketing geniuses!".'

Within a year they were cutting the brewhouse out of Duke's, sticking it in a van and moving it to Hackney Wick. They went from four fermenters to 14 and brewed twice a day but still couldn't make enough beer to keep up with demand. They didn't last a year there before upgrading to their current site in Tottenham Hale, growing from 800 litres a brew to 5,500 with the same eight people.

That was 2014, and since then the growth of the brewery has been a blur even to those documenting it. Going into cans helped Nick's unique designs stand out, and despite growing pains Beavertown's beers have gone from strength to strength. As well as a monster core range they brew regular seasonals that whip beer lovers into a frenzy. In particular, their sticky, bittersweet, glorious mess of a blood orange beer, Bloody 'Ell, is a highlight of the beer calendar. They also now have a barrel store bigger than their original brewery, where they keep their Tempus Project. These aged beers use the final ingredient Logan never had before – time – to extract complexities and subtleties from the wood.

It must all still feel like a dream to Logan, who could never have imagined this kind of success when he made that snap decision over a beer in Brooklyn. Somehow he has managed to remain a rockstar, but this is a much less lonely life. The Sons of Albion could have gone on to great things, but you can sense that this is what Logan was supposed to do with his life. He employs over 80 people now, and seems as in love with them as he is with the beer.

'To get to this stage it was a huge risk. I've never felt so anxious and stressed – I was having heart palpitations and chest pains going through what we did to get here. We did it on a shoestring but we did it right, with excellent people who are now leading the charge. I take a lot of pride in seeing them do that.'

WHERE THE BREWER DRINKS

THIS ONE IS OBVIOUS. BEAVERTOWN STARTED AS A BREWPUB, AND ITS SPECIALS AND FRESHEST BEER IS STILL SERVED AT DUKE'S BREW & QUE ALONG WITH SOME OF THE BEST BARBECUE FOOD IN LONDON. IT'S THE REASON LOGAN STARTED HIS JOURNEY, AND THE PLACE HE ALWAYS GOES BACK TO.

CAMDEN TOWN

CAMDENTOWNBREWERY.COM

**ONE OF THE FIRST WAVE AND SOON TO BE THE BIGGEST,
CAMDEN MAY HAVE MOVED PRODUCTION OUT TO ENFIELD,
BUT A FRESH PINT OF HELLS AT THE OLD TAPROOM IS
STILL A BUCKET-LIST BEER FOR EVERY BEER GEEK.**

Sometimes we forget how tiny most breweries are when they start out. Even the biggest in the world were, at some point, just one guy with a recipe and a lot of plumbing to do. Today, Camden Town Brewery exports all over the world, but in 2007 it was just a naive Aussie and a homebrew kit. Back then Jasper Cuppaidge ran a gastropub called the Horseshoe by Hampstead Tube. It was a nice, gentrified kind of place serving classy pub grub and so-called premium drinks. But like many people at the time, Jasper felt there was something sorely missing. Jasper didn't just see a gap for great British beer, he craved it for himself. With a few technically minded friends from Pitfield Brewery, he built a ramshackle brewhouse in the pub's cellar using old kegs and big saucepans.

'We started with a best bitter if you can believe it. We made Mclaughlin, named after my grandfather, with 100% East Kent Golding hops. That was radical at the time, but I always knew I wanted to make a lager. Obviously the equipment I built didn't allow us to do that though'.

When his beers hit the bar they were an instant hit, being creamy, lively and full-flavoured. More importantly each cask was drunk the same day it was tapped, so that alone was a big step. But for Jasper there were much bigger strides to come.

His ambition to take on the macrobrewers at their own game pushed him to rent four arches beneath Kentish Town West Station and start brewing full time. But, brewing lager is no easy feat because the flavours are so subtle that hiding flaws is impossible. It takes more time in tank, special mashing techniques and world-class ingredients to make something worth selling. This meant that while other new breweries stuck to the kind of kit that Jasper had at the Horseshoe, he had to think a little bigger. Luckily for Jasper, that comes easy to him. The brewery he built was a modern marvel, all shiny chrome tanks and electronic controls. With the scene set, it was time to change lager for good.

WHERE THE BREWER DRINKS

JASPER STILL DRINKS FOUR OR FIVE TIMES A YEAR AT THE WESTBOURNE IN NOTTING HILL. HE CLAIMS TO BE THE BEST GLASS COLLECTOR AT THE BREWERY, AND THIS IS WHERE HE LEARNT THE CRAFT. IT'S MORE THAN NOSTALGIA THOUGH – THE WESTBOURNE HAS A GREAT BEER SELECTION (THOUGH NO CAMDEN) AND IS THE PERFECT PLACE FOR SOMEONE AS BUSY AS JASPER TO UNWIND.

THE LOWDOWN

FOUNDED

2010 (ALTHOUGH BREWING SINCE 2007).

ORIGINS

BREWING REAL ALE IN THE CELLAR OF THE HORSESHOE IN CAMDEN, THE PUB OWNED BY JASPER CUPPAIDGE.

FLAGSHIP BEER

CAMDEN HELLS IS NOW A BRAND IN ITSELF. HALF MALTY, FULL-BODIED PILSNER AND HALF LIGHT, LEMONY HELLES. IT'S SMOOTH AND BREADY BEFORE A BIG BITTER HOP HIT THAT CLEANS THE PALATE. EASILY THE BIGGEST QUALITY LAGER IN THE UK ALTHOUGH IT HAS PLENTY OF COMPETITORS THAT WEREN'T THERE IN 2010. THEIR BEST BEER, HOWEVER, IS IHL – A CROSS BETWEEN A STRONG LAGER AND AN IPA, WITH LOTS OF JUICY FRUIT CHARACTER BUT A LIGHTNING QUICK, CLEAN FINISH.

Jasper picked a recipe halfway between a German pilsner – light, pale and zesty – and more grainy, aromatic Helles.

'The beer was based on what we'd seen on loads of trips to the US and Germany, but inspired by our love of lager in the UK – the body needed to be balanced to be sessionable, but I still wanted texture and a grain character. It was also about double the bitterness of a standard lager because we wanted the hallertau hops at the front. For me it had to be memorable.'

To his credit, I can still remember my first pint of Hells, up at the Horseshoe in 2011. The rest of the world has caught up since, but back then I had never tasted a lager so full-flavoured. It was bready, smooth and somehow fresher. I was a real ale drinker because I never understood the appeal of lager. Now I did.

Countless jaded drinkers must have felt the same, because Camden Town Brewery's growth was phenomenal. The brewing of Hells had to be outsourced to Germany and Belgium to keep up with demand, while the Kentish Town brewery focused on the ales in Jasper's core range. Every Friday, scores of people would turn up at the brewery hoping to buy themselves a pint or six pack. This led to Jasper opening a US-style brewery tap with fresh beer and street food, even hosting parties where beers were served straight from the tanks. Meanwhile he was putting taps in bars all over the capital and beyond – sending bottles back to his native Australia. Demand for a craft British lager was bigger than envisaged.

So I guess we should have seen it coming. From the beginning, Jasper's ambition was to get his lager in every UK pub. For that Camden needed a new brewery,

but to build one big enough would cost tens of millions of pounds. Even in 2015, when banks were finally taking the craft beer business seriously, that kind of capital was hard to come by. In November 2015 it was announced that Camden Town brewery had been sold to megabrewery AB InBev for an enormous £85m.

It provided both the funding and the export markets needed to make the new brewery in Enfield a success but the outcry was damning. In many drinkers' eyes Jasper had turned to the enemy for help. The deal put Camden's delicious Hells, Pils, Pale and IHL next to dire beers like Bud Light and Stella, so the very notion of British craft beer was put to the test. BrewDog tore Camden taps out of their bars with a short, indifferent statement: 'We don't serve beers made by AB InBev.'

Jasper is defiant, still. To him, good lager in every bar is the dream and should be everyone's. Their ability to reach new audiences will help everyone. There are fairer ways to achieve that aim, but you can't argue with the fact that Camden has always been open and honest, helping all smaller breweries and educating drinkers.

'If you look at the brewing scene across the city there are lots of brewers who came from Camden and many have founded pretty damn good breweries,' he says. 'We've always taken ourselves and our beers very seriously and that's become part of the success of the scene.'

That Camden Town Brewery had a huge, positive role to play in the revolution of London beer is without doubt. What role they have in its future remains to be seen. I'll always enjoy a pint of Hells when I'm in Hampstead though, savouring the depth of flavour in the first lager I ever loved.

REDEMPTION

REDEMPTIONBREWING.CO.UK

PERHAPS THE UNSUNG HERO OF THE LONDON CRAFT BEER MOVEMENT, REDEMPTION HAVE BEEN AROUND LONGER THAN ALMOST ANYONE, CONCENTRATING ON THE LESS TRENDY CASK MARKET BUT MAKING BEAUTIFULLY BALANCED, HOP-FORWARD SESSION BEERS.

You only have to go back a decade to find just a handful of breweries in London. We think of the capital as leading the charge in craft beer, but it was actually slow on the uptake. While new breweries like Oakham and Dark Star were trialling hop-forward cask ales in the 1990s, London was turning its breweries into flats and event spaces.

This strange state of affairs was the genesis behind Redemption Brewing, an unashamedly traditional cask brewery. Andy Moffat had been a beer lover and homebrewer for many years and not understood why there weren't more breweries local to London. In 2009, tired of his corporate job and the pressure of recession, he gave it all up to fill what he saw as a gap in the market. As it turns out he wasn't alone. In fact, he was part of the first wave of craft brewers in the capital, setting up in the same year as Sambrook's, Brodie's and The Kernel. Credit crunch aside, it was a great time to

start a brewery, with many of London's new brewers meeting regularly to share beers and help each other out.

'One of my best memories is from the early days, when Phil Lowry [now owner of Dover's Breakwater Brewing] got the few London brewers together for a dinner. Meeting Fuller's John Keeling and Derek Prentice along with Evin O'Riordain – and the subsequent discussions and collaborations which arose – was really special to be part of.'

Where Evin was looking to push the drinkers towards more bitter, citrusy beers, Andy wanted more local breweries in London making exceptional traditional ale.

What seemed like just another British cask brewery at the time quickly became a novel thing, as craft brewing became dominated by kegs. This left Redemption to quietly carve out a niche in cask beer that uses American hops while keeping one eye firmly on British tradition. Redemption cask ales are some of the best in the country. Big Chief, a stunning bittersweet IPA, is a revelation, especially when fresh so the tropical and grassy notes from the New Zealand hops can really sing. But their bread and butter is the session cask ale, with beautifully balanced beers like Hopspur and Trinity making a mockery of much stronger beers with their body and flavour.

While their cask-focused model has kept them out of the more trendy craft beer circles, it has resulted in the kind of brewery that every regular beer drinker is overjoyed to see on the pumps. It may be simple, but the triangular pump clips and colour coding jumps out from the bar, assuring quality and drinkability. There is nothing showy about Redemption and the beers speak for themselves if you give them the chance. Does Andy regret not marketing himself more aggressively?

'We have always focused our resources on the brewing process to the detriment of a marketing budget,' he admits. 'But I think as a brewery, or any business for that matter, you need to balance the need to respond to consumers while staying true to the vision and principles that define you.'

While they haven't grown as fast as some of the companies to come out of the craft beer boom, seven years in they moved to a huge new brewhouse just down the road from Beavertown. This kind of growth in cask ale would have been unthinkable in 2009, let alone back in the seventies when the whole method of dispense was nearly extinct. If bland, fizzy lager is the product that all craft breweries have reacted against, then Redemption's beers are the polar opposite and strongest defence against it.

'When we started, London brewing was mainly discussed in a historical context. Now the capital is appreciated as a centre of modern brewing while still maintaining the culture of heritage and tradition.'

Redemption forms the link between these two worlds; a reminder of the past that's still as relevant as any other brewery in London. For all the advances in beer, real ale still yields the most delicious pints ever made. Cask beer has been lost throughout the world, but it is still very much alive in London and Andy deserves a share of the credit.

THE LOWDOWN

FOUNDED
2009.

ORIGINS
OWNER ANDY MOFFAT SAW A GAP IN THE MARKET, WHEN ONLY FULLER'S WERE MAKING GOOD CASK BEER IN LONDON.

FLAGSHIP BEER
HOPSPUR, NAMED AFTER THE FOOTBALL TEAM LOCAL TO THE BREWERY. A CLASSIC ENGLISH SESSION ALE BUT WITH A BIGGER DOSE OF HOPS THAN YOU'LL FIND FROM OLDER BREWERIES. ENDLESSLY DRINKABLE WITH A WONDERFUL BALANCE BETWEEN HONEY, BISCUIT AND LEMONY PITHINESS.

WHERE THE BREWER DRINKS
GIVEN THE DIRE STATE OF CASK BREWING IN THE CAPITAL WHEN ANDY STARTED, HE'S NOW SPOILT FOR CHOICE AND REFUSES TO GIVE A FAVOURITE PUB. SO LONG AS THE CELLAR IS COLD, THE LINES ARE CLEAN AND THE BEERS ARE REGULARLY CHANGING, HE'S HAPPY.

PUMP CLIP DESIGN

THEY SAY YOU SHOULD NEVER JUDGE A BOOK BY ITS COVER AND THE SAME IS TRUE FOR BEER. THERE ARE SOME WONDERFUL BEERS WRAPPED UP IN TERRIBLE DESIGNS (THE BELGIANS ARE THE WORST FOR IT) AND ALSO SOME ATROCIOUS BEERS WITH BEAUTIFUL BRANDING.

When it comes to beer you should always try before you buy. Sometimes, though, it's hard not to choose the sexiest on the shelf. Beavertown got its big break when people in a local pub all started ordering 'the spaceman beer', and since then they have won as many awards for their space-age designs as their beer. At the other end of the spectrum is The Kernel, which brings drinkers in with its enigmatic, stripped-back brown labels. They couldn't be more different, but both show how craft beer has moved away from the agency-approved insipid stylings of the macrobreweries.

At the same time, most have grown weary of the often sexist and childish branding of some older real ale breweries. Beers like 'Santa's Sack' and 'Easy Blonde', complete with crude cartoon drawings that make any self-respecting drinker cringe, are thankfully becoming a rarity.

Pump clips and beer labels have never been more diverse or exciting, and pubs look all the better for it. It's not just the beer that has got less bland.

ONE MILE END

BREWERY

ONEMILEEND.COM

THEIR TINY WAREHOUSE IN TOTTENHAM IS ABOUT AS CROWDED AND CHAOTIC AS A BREWERY GETS, BUT IT'S FAR MORE PRACTICAL THAN RUNNING UP AND DOWN THE STEPS OF THE WHITE HART PUB'S BASEMENT WHERE THIS BRILLIANT LITTLE BREWERY STARTED.

Music's loss is often beer's gain. There seems to be an affinity between the two, and many brewers have fallen in love with beer after falling out of love with the music industry. It makes a lot of sense. Indie music and craft beer have a lot in common: they are both counter-cultures, rising up against the monopoly of bland, mass-made products; they champion honesty and craft over profit and loss. The morals are paramount, and when someone sells out it's often taken personally. Both industries attract people looking for a lifestyle as much as a career, people who want to create and meet likeminded souls. The most famous example is Logan Plant of Beavertown, who played in the Sons of Albion, but One Mile End's Simon McCabe has a similar story, particularly in finding a love of hops while on the road.

'I used to play in lots of bands but I got tired of worrying about rent and bills,' he says. 'I was looking for a change and I'd toured around America, where I fell in love with hoppy beer. I couldn't find any of it when I got back, so I started brewing it at home.'

In 2010 there were still very few brewers making modern, hop-forward beers, but Redemption had just started up around the corner from his house. Simon gave up the rock'n'roll lifestyle and, in between writing scores for TV shows, began to brew there part-time. As he put it, 'the hobby slowly became a job, and the job became a hobby'. At home he replaced his guitars with brewing equipment, and at Redemption his artistic mind started buzzing. A few years later he met with Patrick Mulligan, who was looking for a new head brewer at his brewpub in Whitechapel. The kit was tiny, even compared to Redemption's, but it offered the freedom someone like Simon needed to express himself.

'I took the job at the White Hart so I could brew what I wanted, and I did 130 different recipes in the first 14 months. They were only two-and-a-half barrel batches so I had nothing to lose really. The majority of them worked but as a brewer I improved a hell of a lot over that time.'

64

With Simon's super-fresh beers hitting the taps just hours after being finished, the pub earned itself a reputation for serving exciting hoppy beer in great condition. Simon seemed to specialise in strong, ultra-pale beers, each one punching you in the face with fruity aroma and pithy bitterness. His IPA, Snake Charmer, and DIPA Snakes Alive stood up among the country's best.

Despite stocking a fair amount of exciting craft beer, everyone was ordering the local stuff on both keg and cask. Word spread and it wasn't long before London publicans started requesting the beer. Demand for Simon's beers grew way beyond the brewery's capacity.

'We were brewing around the clock, six days a week and running the building into tatters – it wasn't designed to be a brewery. We had a lift installed but before that we were carrying kegs and grain bags up narrow stairs too – all for just two barrels of beer at the end of the day.'

Patrick and Simon had agreed to create a new brand for the brewery in the hope that it might one day go solo, but they didn't intend to go commercial as quickly as they did. Fortuitously, Simon's friends at Redemption were looking to upscale and they were able to buy their old six-barrel kit to get started. Moving to Tottenham also heralded the start of their barrel ageing and sour beer programme, including their first ever Gose – a salty German-style beer that they aged on cherries. It seems Simon is not one for standing still despite the huge challenges that come with up-scaling a brewery. Even with a recipe book of around 150 beers and a good reputation earned over years at the pub, the risks were huge. The irony that beer was supposed to be an escape from such worries is not lost on Simon.

'I'd gone full circle and started worrying about bills and rent again,' he laments. 'At the pub I used to hate picking up the phone and having to say we didn't have any beer to sell. Then I got to the big brewery where we were making double the amount straight away, and for the first month I was like 'Where are those phone calls now?!'

Thankfully, since then the phones have been ringing off the hook.

WHERE THE BREWER DRINKS
DESPITE THE EXCITEMENT OF HAVING HIS OWN BREWERY SITE, SIMON MISSES THE WHITE HART, ESPECIALLY FINISHING A SHIFT TO FIND A PINT AND HEARTY FOOD WAITING FOR HIM UPSTAIRS.

HAMMERTON

HAMMERTONBREWERY.CO.UK

AS THE DESCENDENT OF THE BREWER WHO INVENTED THE OYSTER STOUT, LEE HAMMERTON AND HIS YOUNG CRAFT BREWERY HAVE MORE HERITAGE THAN SOME CENTURY-OLD BREWERIES

Hammerton Brewery may be one of the younger breweries on the scene, but you can trace its roots back further than most. Nearly a hundred years further in fact. At first, founder Lee Hammerton has a very familiar story. Bored with his office job and just entering the word of homebrewing, he had begun to nurture dreams of one day having his own brewery. He'd leased a unit, chosen the beers and even bought a brewkit before he got stuck on the brewery name. 'I was actually two months away from opening the brewery before I found out the history and the fact that I was related to the original Hammerton Brewery,' says Lee. 'So believe it or not it was a complete coincidence.'

It turns out that Lee is a descendent of the owners of Charles Hammerton & Co, a brewery in Stockwell, which was closed in 1964 after being bought out by Watneys. They had been brewing in London since 1730, meaning beer has been in Lee's blood for nearly 300 years. Despite being averse to naming his brewery after himself, this was too serendipitous to ignore.

'My brother had found the name and bought some badges off eBay, but it was only when I visited my grandparents and told them I was starting a brewery that they told me that we were actually relatives. I then had to get the trademark revoked from Heineken to use it, but that's another story.'

The name wasn't the only bit of history Lee borrowed when opening the brewery. The original Hammerton is often credited as the first brewer of oyster stout – which as you may guess is a dark, roasty beer made with live oysters. This legend is made all the more exciting by the fact that the origins are still disputed. Some say Hammerton was the first, and that stout and oysters were not combined until then but enjoyed together because during the Industrial Revolution they were working-class treats. But brewing records have also found use of the shells as finings to reduce cloudiness in the beer before then.

Either way, Hammerton were likely the first to use them in the actual brewing process, something

Lee was keen to play upon. Despite his intention to make modern, hop-forward beers, Pentonville stout was one of the first beers he produced, made with whole oysters.

'After doing a fair bit of research on the style of beer and research on oysters in general, we decided to use Wild Oysters from the Blackwater Estuary. We order them fresh from the oyster farmers there and they are picked fresh from the Estuary and delivered about 11am. By 1pm they are boiling away in the kettle.'

It sounds confusing and unappetising, but the oysters merely add a little salt and minerality to the beer, which help to make it a much more rounded and full-bodied stout. Far from being a gimmick beer, it is one of the most drinkable and satisfying dark beers being made in London. Unless you're allergic to fish.

Pentonville wasn't the only surprise hit from

Hammerton. Many know them for cask ales, but that wasn't their intention either. They were actually victims of their own success, winning awards for their pale ale, N1, and IPA, N7. Both these golden ales are fantastic fresh on cask, with a perfect balance between sweet, golden-syrup-like malts and bitter, grapefruity hops. This brought them huge success and pushed them to produce over 500,000 pints of them in 2016. But such a reputation also meant their taproom got so busy that their more experimental brews were drunk before they could escape the brewery – beers like Baron H, their Earl Grey black IPA, and Chicha Pale, made with Purple Peruvian Corn.

You get a sense in talking to Lee and drinking his beer that there is a lot more to come from Hammerton. Much of what they have done is rooted in history and tradition, but there is a bright future ahead.

THE LOWDOWN

FOUNDED

2014.

ORIGINS

FOUNDED BY BORED OFFICE WORKER LEE HAMMERTON, WHO WANTED TO FOUND A LOCAL BREWERY IN THE HEART OF ISLINGTON. HE LATER DISCOVERED HIS OWN BREWING ROOTS IN CHARLES HAMMERTON & CO. BREWING.

BRILLIANT BECAUSE

THEY HAVE DEMONSTRATED A RESPECT FOR THE PAST, BUT HAVE A UNIQUE WAY OF LOOKING AT IT WITH THEIR ADJUNCT BREWING AND BRILLIANT CASK ALES.

FLAGSHIP BEER

PENTONVILLE. BY NO MEANS THEIR BESTSELLING BEER, BUT IT SHOWS THEIR PRIDE IN LONDON AND FAMILY BREWING, AS WELL AS QUITE A BIT OF DARING WHEN IT COMES TO RELEASING UNUSUAL BEERS.

WHERE THE BREWER DRINKS

LEE KEEPS IT LOCAL TO ISLINGTON, ENJOYING THE AWESOME SUNDAY ROAST AT THE ALMA, AND SIPPING ON MORE UNUSUAL BEERS AT THE EARL OF ESSEX AND CRAFT BEER CO ON WHITE LION STREET.

NAME	STYLE	CASK KEG	ABV	HALF PINT	PINT	BOTTLE	
1	N1	SESSION PALE ALE	KEG	4.1%	£2.20	£4.40	✓	TAPROOM
2	PENTONVILLE	OYSTER STOUT	KEG	5.3%	£2.30	£4.60	✓	
3	BARON H	BLACK EARL-GREY IPA	KEG	5.8%	£2.30	£4.60	✓	
4	BLANK SLATE	TABLE PALE	KEG	3.2%	£2.10	£4.20	✓	
5	ISLINGTON	UNFILTERED LAGER	KEG	4.7%	£2.10	£4.20	✓	
6	CHICHA	PERUVIAN CHICHA PALE	KEG	4.5%	£2.30	£4.60		NEXT
7	N7	INDIAN PALE ALE	KEG	5.2%	£2.30	£4.60	✓	
8	MÄRZEN	GERMAN MARCH BEER	KEG	5.1%	£2.20	£4.40		
9								

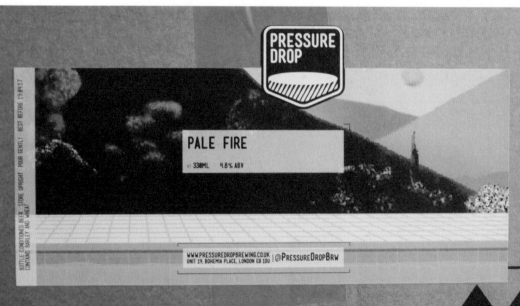

PRESSURE DROP

PRESSUREDROPBREWING.CO.UK

A TINY BREWERY WITH A BIG REPUTATION, PRESSURE DROP
WOWED THE CAPITAL WITH THEIR FLAGSHIP BEER, PALE FIRE,
AND THE BEER HAS SENT THEM ON A JOURNEY NONE OF THE
FOUNDERS EVER CONCEIVED IN THEIR WILDEST DREAMS.

Looking at the beautiful bottles and tasting the beer, you'd be forgiven for thinking Pressure Drop was a much bigger brewery than it is. In fact, until recently they were a tiny outfit down a potholed street by Hackney Central. Decorated with old mattresses, burning oil drums and abandoned cars, it's not the kind of place you'd expect to find an artisan anything, let alone a brewery. But it was there, in a railway arch far from the relative glamour of the Bermondsey Beer Mile, that Pressure Drop decided to set up shop.

Founded by three avid homebrewers, they have built a brilliant reputation and brand while handling all the brewing, cleaning, sales, accounts and deliveries themselves. Asking them how they managed this is

pointless because they are as surprised as anyone.

'We just started in Graham's shed with a little homebrew kit,' says Sam Smith. 'We made the odd drinkable beer – Wugang was the second or third beer we ever brewed and it hasn't really changed – but it was for us to drink back then. I guess there was a plan there, but usually the good beers were accidental.'

They like to say that things happen by chance, but as the old idiom goes, you make your own luck and Pressure Drop have a habit of being in the right place at the right time. Graham O'Brien and Sam had known each other since school, meeting Ben Freeman while helping out at London Fields Brewery. They had been hanging out with the London Amateur Brewers society,

---

WHERE THE BREWER DRINKS
MOTHER KELLYS AND THE KINGS ARMS GET PRESSURE DROP'S VOTES AS BEST FOR SOMETHING NEW AND
EXCITING, BUT THEY ALSO LOVE THE CHESHAM ARMS FOR A GREAT COMMUNITY PUB VIBE.

which at that point still counted the Kernel's Evin O'Riordain as a member. They timed their founding perfectly, making the leap to commercial brewers just behind the likes of Brew By Numbers and Beavertown, when interest in the craft beer movement was starting to pick up. Unusually, though, their beer list wasn't rammed with hops and high abvs. They had taken a very different, London-centric approach that set them apart. By accident, of course.

'I don't think that first range was that deliberate,' says Graham. 'It was just a case that those were the best beers we had. If we'd produced an IPA we were happy with we'd have released that. We weren't like "we have to have this and that", although I think the pale ale was one we wanted, just so we could drink it.'

The beer Graham is referring to is Pale Fire, still one of the best session pales in the country and so well known that some people think it's the name of the brewery. It has such international acclaim that they have to put Japanese signage outside the brewery for the tourists. It has a gorgeous, soft, overripe mango aroma

and, thanks to the addition of wheat, a smooth, soft body that still finishes crisp and light. It was a beautifully balanced beer in a time when most brewers were pushing bitterness to the max. That softer approach has been a gateway to craft beer for thousands of drinkers. Like yoyos and Pogs when we were kids, Pale Fire was the thing everybody wanted back in 2014.

'The response and the demand for the beer took us by surprise,' says Ben. 'We talk about it a lot – what we did differently – because it takes up half our tank space now. There was no plan to build a beer that was also a brand. It just happened.'

'I guess it's because we're different to many breweries in that we do everything ourselves,' adds Graham. 'We're three brewers and we developed the business around that. Through brewing Pale Fire we decided that what's important to us is the best ingredients, and there's no outside pressure saying "Those hops are too expensive". We all understand it.'

While Pale Fire occupies most of their tank space, it has allowed them to be more eccentric with their other beers. They make a selection of big IPAs (Alligator Tugboat is a standout beer) but also some that are almost wilfully obscure. They admit that their smoked wheat beer, Freimann's Dunkelweiss, 'isn't everyone's idea of fun', while Strictly Roots is a quirky dandelion and burdock porter made with foraged roots from the Hackney Marshes. Unsurprisingly, they get fewer Japanese tourists asking for that one.

When someone sets up a new small business, it's amazing what they find inside themselves – a head for spreadsheets, an eye for design, or a shrewd marketing instinct. A bit of all of those things reside in the three founders, but you wouldn't know it to look at them. A dab hand at plumbing, sure, but even they seem entirely nonplussed by the image they have created. Looking at their branding you can see the flaws – the brewery name is hidden, the beer's explanation tiny and the images often abstract. By breaking all the rules they've found a cohesive personality that shines from every bottle. This is all the more remarkable given that the labels are made by disparate artists, photographers and collaborators.

None of it should work but it does, and it's no accident, whatever they claim. They have just started brewing at a new site up in Tottenham Hale, adding to the exciting brewing community already there. The bigger site means we're going to be seeing a lot more Pale Fire around the country, while they can convert the old site into a pilot brewery or taproom. What happens next, no one knows, least of all Ben, Sam and Graham.

'When I first started thinking about starting a brewery I was working in the Euston Tap,' says Graham. 'I asked a few people what they thought and some said, "This craft thing is getting out of hand now. There's like 10 breweries in London". Now there's over 90. No one could guess where it's going, and long may that continue.'

THE LOWDOWN

FOUNDED
2012.

ORIGINS
THREE HOMEBREWERS, ONE SHED, ONE DREAM.

BRILLIANT BECAUSE
THEY MAKE EXACTLY THE KIND OF BEER THEY WANT TO DRINK, WITH NO STRATEGY OR MOTIVE. NO ELSE ONE COULD PRODUCE THE KIND OF SMALL-BATCH, LOCALLY-INSPIRED BEERS THEY SPECIALISE IN. THEY FORAGE FOR INGREDIENTS, RECREATE OLD STYLES AND FOCUS ON THE LOCAL MARKET.

FLAGSHIP BEER
THE AMAZING PALE FIRE. STILL ONE OF THE BEST PALE ALES MADE IN THE UK, IT SINGS WITH SOFT OVERRIPE FRUITS AND HAS A SOFT, SMOOTH BODY THAT MAKES IT ENDLESSLY DRINKABLE.

SOUTH

LONDON

SOUTH LONDON IS RARELY SEEN AS THE HIP PART OF TOWN. EVEN THE TUBE IS TOO COOL TO GO TO MOST OF IT. BUT IT IS GROUND ZERO FOR THE REVIVAL OF GOOD BEER IN THE CITY, MAYBE THE COUNTRY.

It's been well over a decade since Meantime brewed its first batch in Greenwich, hailing the start of the keg beer revolution in the UK. America may be the main influence in the rise of British craft beer, but it was a classically German-trained brewer who first waved that flag. Alastair Hook's beers were varied and full of something that most beer drinkers weren't used to – flavour. Even his lager had the bittersweetness of a German Helles, setting it apart from countless brands.

Sadly, Meantime beers have not stood the test of time particularly well, but the revolution has spread to more daring breweries chasing innovation rather than volume. The heartland of London craft brewing moved slightly west to Bermondsey, where an equally inspirational man saw the magic of American IPAs and was adamant the UK needed to see the light too. In a small railway arch he started brewing hop-forward, hazy beers that flouted all the rules British brewing had enshrined over 50 years. In the shadows of one of the UK's busiest train lines, small artisan businesses were growing in closed garages and carwashes – bakers, butchers, jam makers and brewers.

Former cheese maker Evin O'Riordain is the one who

started it all. An unassuming man, especially compared to his beers, which are a riot of colour and flavour, he is the perfect role model for new breweries – experimental, artisan to his core and never, ever boastful. His only ambition is to make the best beer he can. He and the other Bermondsey brewers are leading the charge in small-batch, exciting beers and are well known for working together to keep pushing the boundaries.

Within a square mile you'll find Brew By Numbers, Partizan, Anspach & Hobday, Southwark and Fourpure. Every one except Kernel opens on a Saturday for the 'Bermondsey Beer Mile', a crawl of epic proportions that proves too much for many. The stag-dos aren't used to such strong and varied beer and towards the end of the afternoon it looks like a scene from *28 Days Later*. But come Monday, it is back to brewing – a business that has changed the fortunes of the area.

Next time you take a journey out of London Bridge don't think about the destination or the delays. Think about how five metres below you, in barrels, fermenters, bottles, casks, cans and kegs, some of the best beer in the world is being made.

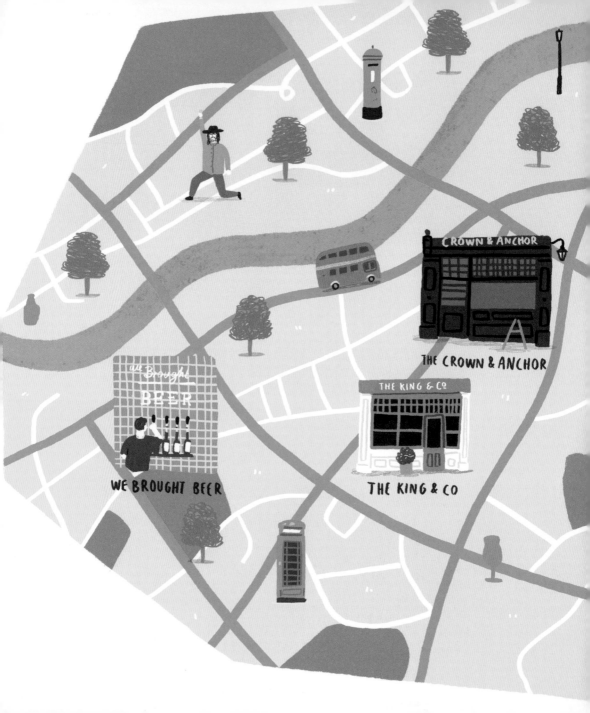

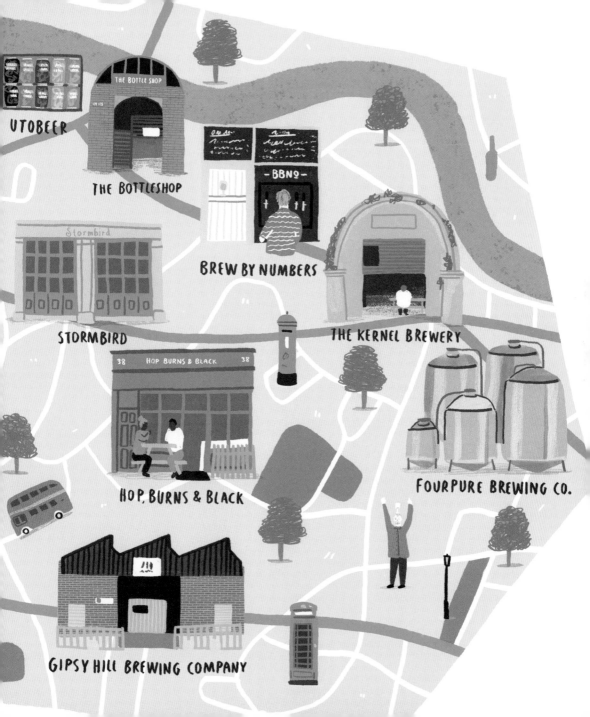

THE KING & CO

THEKINGANDCO.UK

PRETTY MUCH THE ONLY PUB OR BAR IN CLAPHAM WORTH VISITING
FOR BEER LOVERS, THIS LOVELY LOCAL HAS A GREAT BEER LIST,
FASCINATING DÉCOR AND SOME GREAT POP-UP KITCHEN FOOD.

There are the ghosts of all kinds of things at King & Co. The pub has been through endless reincarnations over its long life, going from a giant pub on two floors to the more modest one it is now, through eras known as the King's Head, Smokerooms, Grey Goose and 100 Club. The pub and its landlord, Anthony Gunson, have absorbed lots of history and lots of what's great about other pubs. Today it stands proud and modern in the less showy part of Clapham, worlds away from the soulless cocktail bars of the main strip. Its high ceilings emphasise how big the place is, but it never feels cold or empty. A three-sided bar dominates the room, where a bright King & Co sign illuminates the vast spirits and wine selection. The beer selection is just as wide, with 14 keg lines and four cask beers that take in most of London and a fair amount of the world too.

The walls are scattered with memorabilia but it's done with a lot more precision than in most pubs – artfully placed clock faces and mirrors have something fairytale about them, the kind of wall you might find in a C S Lewis book. Elsewhere, old photos picked up at an antique fair show historic scenes of Clapham, and the beer board that sports so many modern beers is itself antique. The décor's slightly fussy nature matches the landlord.

'Yeah the design is pretty much all me,' says Anthony. 'I'm not happy with it at this point but I never have been. We've been here two years and we've already redecorated twice.'

If you have the time to take it all in you'll be left wondering what he could possibly improve. It's not

BEERS	14 KEG LINES, 4 CASK, SOME DECENT BOTTLES.
CULTURE	A MIX OF OLD, YOUNG, TRENDY AND NERDY. DIFFERENT EVERY TIME, AND THAT'S KIND OF THE CHARM.

all for show, the little nuances make The King & Co
a very comfortable place to drink. A small coal fire
with armchairs glows invitingly in the winter, and in
summer the revelry spills out into the courtyard and the
merriment drowns out the traffic from the main road.

Being on a main route has its benefits. The King & Co
is part of an emerging Clapham craft beer scene. Along
with a few other good pubs they form what (a few) people
call Route 37. Technically a bus route, it's a line of good
watering holes that ends at the excellent bottle shop We

Brought Beer, where you have a celebratory pint, fill
your boots then head home to crack open a few more. It
doesn't end there, as a few breweries are opening up in the
vicinity too, and Anthony likes to wave the Clapham flag
whenever he can. It's a testament to the depth of London
brewing that his favourite brewery is one I have hardly
ever seen on tap anywhere else in London.

'We have a very close relationship with London Beer
Lab, just down the road. They make our house ale, Little
Hopster, a 3.8% pale ale which my bar manager brews

with the guys. It's his recipe and he's a keen homebrewer.'

Aside from the house beer, everything on tap is on quick rotation, and it's not the only thing constantly changing. Rather than hiring a chef and playing around with menus, Anthony simply invites a street food vendor in to do a pop-up kitchen. Gourmet tapas lovers Donostia are the house favourites, but the kitchen changes hands a few times a year to keep the locals interested and help inspire events and the beer selection. When we were last in they had a few Basque beers on to match the Spanish food. It's a simple idea but it encourages people to try new things.

'I think we were the first to do it and people are following us now – realising that the traditional model for a pub can change. There are different angles you can take within it to make something more interesting.'

In a part of London famous for serving magnums of Dom Perignon to city slickers, The King & Co is a beacon of beer striking out on its own. We expect Route 37 to get a whole lot busier.

CASK ALES +
HAND-PULL CIDER

BRIGHTON BIER -5% | £5.50
No NAME STOUT

LITTLE HOPSTER -3.8% | £3.80
PALE ALE

MANCHESTER BREWING Co.
CUT LIKE A BUFFALO APA

ELUSIVE BREWING 4.2% | £4.40
ENGLISH PALE ALE

ELUSIVE BREWING 5.3% | £4.70
AMERICAN PA

SEACIDER
MARMALADE

THE BOTTLE SHOP

BOTTLESHOP.CO.UK

THE GO-TO PLACE FOR RARE AND EXCITING AMERICAN IMPORTS, AS WELL AS SOME SPECIALIST STUFF FROM EUROPE. YOU'RE DRINKING IN A WAREHOUSE AND YOU'RE WELL AWARE OF IT, BUT WHEN THE BEER IS THIS GOOD NO ONE SEEMS TO CARE.

Ten years ago there is no way people would have turned up at a cold, cramped distribution warehouse for a night out. Now it is the norm. Until recently The Bottle Shop was the headquarters of a craft beer importing company, shipping out pallets across the country every day. Finding themselves near the start of London's coolest new bar crawl, the company trialled opening on Saturdays and pouring some of their nerdier beers. It was uncomfortable, improvised and so cramped that you resorted to resting your pint on a forklift. So its success took everyone by surprise, including the owners.

The Bottle Shop's story starts with one man, a fridge and a till in Canterbury, set up in a converted shunting railway shed. The founder, Andrew Morgan, was stocking his little shop by buying delicious beers from all over the world. For one man, that wasn't cheap, but he kept costs down by buying in bulk and sharing it with other local businesses. That tiny wholesale operation took off, and after a few lock ups ended up

in Bermondsey, through knowing some of the artisan businesses springing up there.

'It was very much a warehouse, with two taps of beer and some takeaway to help pay the rent,' says Peter Brissenden, head of south-east sales at The Bottle Shop and renowned beer blogger. 'But within a year, the amount of space we needed was throttling our wholesale growth. I remember 13 pallets of Mikkeller arriving one day, out in the road blocking traffic, and our warehouse manager with no idea where it was going to go.'

They hastily installed a mezzanine bar area – where the low curved roof makes it feel like an air raid shelter – and since getting a larger warehouse out in Canning Town they have been slowly converting the downstairs into an epic, er… bottle shop.

It still stretches the notion of a pub to the very extreme, but the beer lists each week are enough to make the most jaded beer lover run straight out of his house in his jammies and head there on Saturday

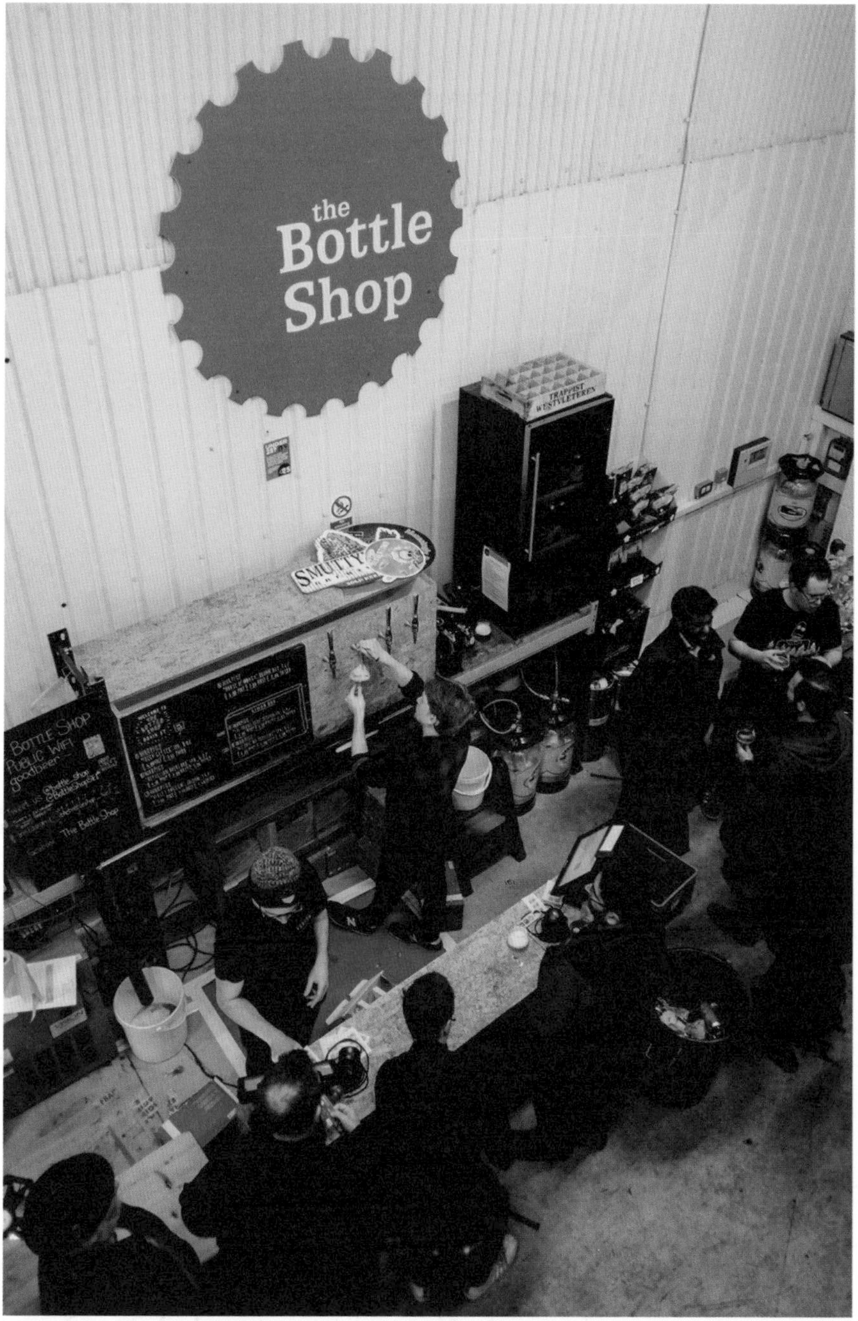
the Bottle Shop

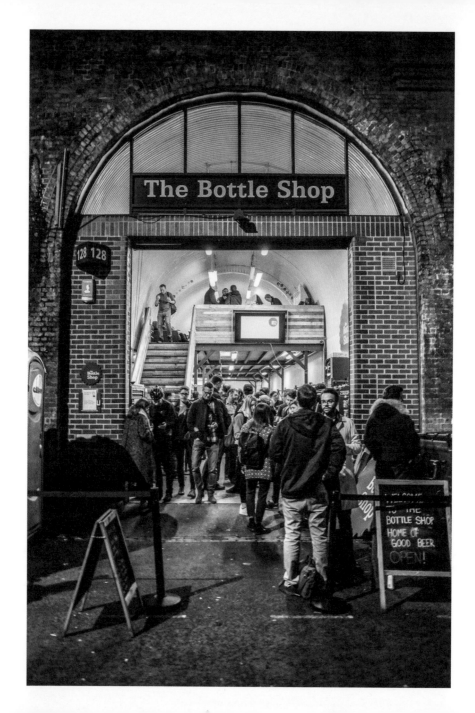

morning. As the importers they get first pick on some very rare and exciting stuff. They get regular containers from the US West Coast, rammed with the best beer they can get their hands on. In particular you should watch out for anything from Monkish, Almanac and Crooked Stave, all of whom make stunning sour and fruited beers that don't suffer from the 5,000-mile journey like IPAs do. Every month they also receive a few pallets of Swedish sensation Omnipollo, who make some of the world's most experimental beers from hazy hopbombs to stouts imbued with ice-cream flavours. Releases of these rarities have caused queues come opening time.

'Last April 1st was a Friday and we put 14 lines of Omnipollo on at the arch and genuinely had people messaging us asking "Is this an April Fool's joke? Do you honestly have those beers on draught?" Any time we get it in the shop is just bonkers.'

If you don't fancy fighting through the crowds, the upstairs bomb shelter is frequently the home of exciting ticketed events. Sometimes it's a food and beer night, sometimes a meet the brewer, and sometimes simply

a bottleshare where they crack their rarest bottles for groups to try. These nights can be pretty special, and give you the warm glow of thinking you know one of London's best-kept secrets. You don't, of course, as the crowds attest come Saturday afternoon, but most of those drinkers don't realise they are in the bar that stocks all the great pubs in London. So get there early and browse the incredible shelves and fridges before settling in with a pint or two; you'll be amazed at what you can find.

BEERS	FOURTEEN TAPS, ENDLESS SHELVES AND EVER-INCREASING FRIDGES THAT GROAN WITH RARE BEER. THE BEERS' ORIGINS VARY SO MUCH THOUGH THAT IF YOU'RE AFTER SOMETHING SPECIFIC, IT'S BEST TO CHECK VIA SOCIAL MEDIA BEFORE MAKING THE JOURNEY.
CULTURE	THE ARCH HAS A GREAT, RELAXED FEEL ON A FRIDAY AS BEER NERDS AND 'WHALE HUNTERS' BOND OVER FINDING THE RAREST BOTTLES. ON SATURDAY THERE'S MUCH MORE OF A PARTY ATMOSPHERE, WITH THE TAPS FLOWING AND FRIDGES FLYING OPEN. I LIKE TO FINISH THERE AFTER A TRIP DOWN THE MILE BECAUSE THE SHEER VARIATION IS HARD TO LEAVE BEHIND IF YOU HIT IT AT THE START.

STORMBIRD

THESTORMBIRDPUB.CO.UK

NO PUB IN LONDON CAN COMPETE WITH THE WILD AND EXCITING BEERS THAT STORMBIRD PUTS ON – BEERS SO RARE THEY DON'T EVEN HAVE TAP BADGES – AND THE FRIDGES GROAN UNDER THE WEIGHT OF HARD-TO-FIND BOTTLES AND CANS.

A quiet evening in Stormbird is a bit like being in a goldfish bowl. The tall windows look straight out onto a busy A road, but it somehow feels like another world. You see but you don't hear the traffic through the single glazing – even sirens make no noise as they flash past. The calm inside is complete. Far from the offices of central London, week nights start slow at Stormbird. People sit and whisper to each other, as if scared of sending ripples across the water. The staff are quiet too, floating around behind the bar, patiently telling almost every customer who drifts in that it's cash only but there's a cash machine round the corner. Acoustic heartbreakers play through the speakers and you can physically feel yourself relax into the mismatched, rugged furniture.

This timeless feel isn't what you'd expect given the pub's reputation as a craft beer destination. It should be heaving with young trendsetters, carrying their Casio synths and shouting about beard oil. It's almost as if

these people don't actually like good beer: if they did they'd be here, ruining it for everyone.

You see, the beer list goes way beyond your average craft beer bar. There's a hell of a lot of thought behind Stormbird's selection, and no small amount of fearlessness too. The tap list starts with a few well-known craftier beers – Goose Island, Dark Star, Beavertown – before sliding off the scales in obscurity with B-side Mikkeller beers and Partizan draught barely seen outside the brewery. Most of the beers are so ephemeral they don't even have tap badges, just hastily hand-drawn notes with the name and ABV. To serve so many unusual beers would be brave in the busiest of pubs, but out in Camberwell it seems foolhardy. On one occasion I asked what lagers they had on, to which they replied, 'none'. In most pubs, lagers account for well over half the sales.

The remarkable list doesn't stop there. Together with the 20-strong tap list comes about 60 fridge beers

that require help navigating even for the initiated. Casually scrawled on the doors are the vague styles of the beers, ranging from stouts to sours, but it's easy to get hopelessly lost in the myriad colours, fonts, images and shapes. I've seen Cloudwater DIPA, Buxton Yellow Belly, Omnipollo Anagram and a whole host of other seriously rare and expensive beers. There's no fanfare, they just sit there on the shelf next to everything else. You can see people stop in their tracks as they scan the fridges, wondering if it's some kind of trick. But there is no trick to Stormbird, as founder Maura Gannon proves.

'I had run tied pubs with my dad for years, and we were frustrated with the selection, given our love of US and Belgian beers. When a premises became available near us I just went for it, and now it's hard not to have a good selection. Given my past in tied pubs I'm still like a kid in a sweetshop!'

It feels like that to me too, but it's also just a local village pub that happens to have a beer list bigger than all of West London combined. Mauna knows what people like, but also what they need. It is the only pub I know that has a gluten-free beer menu, where all casks are £3 a pint, and they'll give a discount if you want to take a few bottles home with you. Which you will.

| **BEERS** | ABSOLUTELY INSANE – 20 WELL-CHOSEN TAPS (AND USUALLY ONE CASK LINE) PLUS OVER 100 BOTTLES AND CANS. ON OCCASION YOU'LL FIND SOMETHING VERY RARE INDEED, SO MAKE SURE YOU SCAN THE FRIDGES AND ASK QUESTIONS OF THE BARSTAFF SO YOU DON'T MISS A ONCE-IN-A-LIFETIME BEER. | **CULTURE** | QUIET AND CONSIDERED – SOMETIMES A BIT LIKE A LIBRARY – BUT IT GROWS INCREASINGLY ROWDY AS THE NIGHTS GO ON. IF MEETING FRIENDS I LIKE TO ARRIVE EARLY TO NURSE A PINT AND SOAK UP THE CALM BEFORE THE STORM(BIRD). |

SOUTH LONDON • Stormbird

THE CROWN & ANCHOR

PUB

WWW.CROWNANDANCHORBRIXTON.CO.UK

A GIANT, AIRY PUB THAT HAS A SPECIAL LINE IN UNEXPECTED CASK ALES AND CLICHÉD AMERICAN BAR FOOD. SOUNDS AWESOME, RIGHT?

There aren't many reasons to visit this part of London but The Crown & Anchor is chief among them. To most, Stockwell is just a point where the Northern and Victoria lines cross and tired commuters traipse from one platform to the other, coming together like bumper cars. Leave the tube and head towards the pub, however, and Stockwell reveals hidden grandeur and a pub that neatly dissects the crawl between the King & Co and Stormbird.

Its sister site, the Jolly Butchers, was one of the first true craft beer pubs in London. But east London is now spoilt for choice and the pub up in Stoke Newington is just one among many. The Crown & Anchor has no such issue, and can spread its wings safe in the knowledge that, as Stockwell dwellers make their way home, plenty of them will have the sense to stop off.

Which is lucky because the pub is huge. It's noticeable how much more space pubs south of the river seem to have. Where most London pubs are crammed into terrace buildings and odd-shaped corners, Bermondsey and Southwark pubs take all the space they

need. Long and thin like a train carriage, The Crown & Anchor stretches the entire length of the side street that connects the A23 to the Slade Gardens park. Picnic tables line the pedestrianised road and get seriously busy come summer, while takeaway cans for the park do a roaring trade too. The bar counter nearly makes it the whole way down the building but peters out towards the end. It's lined with stools in the American way, so those at the bar can order without having to leave their seats but everyone else has to hover awkwardly behind them, waving their arms to get attention.

Other than the vast space it feels a lot like the Jolly Butchers, with lots of exposed brick and ironwork. It's not cosy but it is comfortable and buzzy – somewhere close to the true meaning of hygge. On the walls behind the bar are neon and tin signs that declare the place defiantly craft. Don't be put off if you are looking for something more adventurous than the lit-up Brooklyn Brewery though. The keg taps are loaded with British specials from Wild, Wiper & True and other smaller producers. The cask is well cared for with some lovely

BEERS	THIRTEEN KEGS OF WELL-CHOSEN BRITISH AND AMERICAN, PLUS TEN CASK LINES. IGNORE THE STIEGL AS THERE ARE USUALLY BETTER LAGERS IN THE FRIDGES.
CULTURE	BUSY BUT NEVER OVERCROWDED DURING THE WEEK (IT'S A BIG PLACE TO FILL). DURING THE WEEKEND TABLES ARE HARD TO COME BY BUT ARE WORTH IT FOR THE FRESHLY COOKED, CLASSIC PUB GRUB.

choices like Marble Pint and the odd Salopian beer, a very underrated brewery rarely seen in London. There are occasionally some American beers too, but the local stuff is always fresher and better priced here. If nothing seasonal impresses, it's also one of the few places in London to get a pint of BrewDog Punk IPA without having to be sat on an unforgiving stool and assaulted with craft propaganda.

On top of that they still have (at the time of writing) a Hopinator, a method of dispense that allows you to infuse beers as you pour them. The equipment was originally designed to be used with hops, but given the limited time that the liquid sees the hops it made almost no difference, so ill-advised experiments with everything from strawberries to cocoa beans were conducted. It leaves a perfectly good beer at the mercy of the barman (so always try it before committing to a pint) but after a few liveners it's always worth a go.

Once you're stranded in a place like Stockwell, food might be required. There's a fantastic Indian and craft beer kitchen opposite, but if you're too lazy The Crown & Anchor kitchen menu reads like an Americana greatest hits album. Burgers, hot dogs, pulled pork and nachos, all with a British bent that makes you feel like you're still in a British pub. Together with the decent beer, wine and spirit list, this place is about as edgy as you can get while still being an option for Sunday lunch with the parents. Depending on your point of view, that's pretty much exactly what you want a traditional pub to be.

HOP, BURNS & BLACK

PUB

HOPBURNSBLACK.CO.UK

A BRILLIANT LITTLE BOTTLESHOP AND THE ONLY ONE TO
MAKE OUR SHORTLIST THANKS TO THE ABILITY TO DRINK IN
AND THE UTTERLY UNIQUE SELECTION OF DELICIOUS NEW
ZEALAND BOTTLES BROUGHT IN BY THE KIWI OWNERS.

Hop, Burns & Black may sound more like a law firm than a beer shop, but it happens to be one of the best in the country and these days that's quite an honour. The unusual name comes from the fact that they actually sell hot sauce and vinyl as well as great beer.

'We call them the "three greatest obsessions", together at last,' says Jen Ferguson, who founded the shop with her partner Glenn Williams in 2014. 'Someone once said if you do what you love it doesn't feel like work, which sounded pretty good to us. Then once we had the idea for a beer shop, we thought, why not surround ourselves with the other things we love?'

Surrounded is the right word. Bottles cover the store's walls higher than you can reach even behind the counter. They're not just for takeaway though, as the picnic bench outside implies, you can drink on site, which means customers can crack one beer open while deciding what else to take home.

That can take a while because Jen and Glenn have fine taste and well over 350 beers to peruse. Sometimes

BEERS	OVER 350 BOTTLES IN THE FRIDGES AND TWO TAPS FOR FLAGON FILLS, MOSTLY FROM THE UK BUT WITH PLENTY OF FOCUS ON EUROPE AND AMERICA, AS WELL AS RARITIES FROM NEW ZEALAND.
CULTURE	VERY RELAXED AND CANTEEN-LIKE, WITH EVERYONE SHARING TABLES AND STORIES. WATCH OUT FOR THE EVENTS THAT HAPPEN EVERY FEW MONTHS, USUALLY WITH A LOCAL BEER CELEB HOSTING.

I'm on my second beer before I've filled my basket. They buy in the best London breweries, as well as all the good stuff from the 2,000 other breweries around the UK. On top of that they have a healthy imported list from America, Belgium, Scandinavia and their native New Zealand.

'I first moved to London in 2000 and knew I'd found home,' says Jen. 'I returned to New Zealand in late 2005 for what was supposed to be a one-year sojourn but met Glenn. We arrived back just before the 2012 Olympics, which was an amazing time to introduce someone to London. Glenn was like "Wow, so friendly!" and I said "Don't get used to it".'

Despite moving to London in part for the beer, the pair bring in a lot of beers from their homeland that no other bottleshop can. Some of them are brilliant too, no worse for wear after the long journey. I've had fantastic bottles of Panhead and Hop Federation at the events I've attended there. Jen and Glenn are a key part of the London craft beer scene and hold regular tastings, talks and podcast recordings at the shop. That means every few weeks the shop gets absolutely rammed with beer writers, brewers and the odd sheepish shopper who's not quite sure what's going on.

'There's something quite lovely about the intimacy of it all. Because we're a shop, not a bar, we only have limited seating so people usually have to share tables. I love looking out on a sunny afternoon and seeing a bunch of strangers becoming friends. We've met some of our favourite people through serving them great beer.'

You certainly don't see the same socialising in a Tesco's booze aisle and it's heartening to see it for yourself too. People have been brought together by beer, or in some cases hot sauce, and leave not just with a basket full of beer but a new drinking buddy. You can see the pride Jen and Glenn take in creating a tiny social hub in an unlikely part of south London. It's what running an independent, artisan business is all about and you see it across all London's craft beer pubs and shops.

'There's a real sense of camaraderie in the scene, whether you're a brewer, a beer seller or a beer lover,' says Jen. 'I think that support is going to be invaluable in the years ahead as the big multi-nationals try to muscle in on the act. We're all in this together.'

BERMONDSEY BEER MILE

WHEN I PICTURE MORNINGS ON DRUID STREET, I LIKE TO THINK OF THE RISING SUN GLINTING OFF A DISTANT CANARY WHARF, THE SOUND OF BIRDS SINGING, THE ODD BAGUETTE-CARRYING CYCLIST WHISTLING ON THEIR WAY HOME FOR BREAKFAST.

———

I don't actually know what happens because, like everyone else, I turn up at midday when the railway arch shutters roll up. That's when this seemingly run-down backstreet transforms into the most vibrant brewing street anywhere in the world. This square mile of Bermondsey is home to countless food producers, two street markets and seven craft breweries. Among them is the grandfather of London craft, The Kernel, as well as an 'open brewery' where you can make beer yourself.

Every Saturday, come rain or shine, flavour crusaders flock to the arches just after London Bridge station to drink in the breweries' taprooms. Like any food- or drink-based activity in London, it draws big crowds and has a buzzing, excitable atmosphere. It has also gained a reputation for being the target of stag and hen dos – Tom of Brew By Numbers swears he once saw a stag towing a handcuffed dwarf (apparently both were barred entry) – but in many ways that just adds to the colour.

Towards the end of the day it can resemble a zombie B-flick as much as a food and drink market, but come early and you will be rewarded with some of the best artisan food and drink in the country in a buzzing environment.

BREW BY NUMBERS

BREWBYNUMBERS.COM

WALKING INTO THE BREWERY YOU JUST KNOW THE BEER IS GOING TO
BE GOOD. IT'S CHAOTIC AND EXCITING, BUBBLING AND OVERFLOWING
WITH IDEAS JUST LIKE THEIR HAZY, HOP-FORWARD BEERS.

Near the back of Brew by Numbers' chaotic arch there are two tall fermenting tanks. The first is called James Brown and the second Rick James. On one level the names describe the two different kinds of 'funky' yeast fermentation going on in each tank, but on another level they explain a lot about Brew by Numbers. They are complete nerds.

Founded by Dave Seymour and Tom Hutchings, the brewery takes its name from the numbering system the pair used in their homebrew days to remember which beers were in which fermenting bucket. They liked to play around with different yeasts and hops, so often had several recipes bubbling away at any one time. The Brew by Numbers system was simple: the first number indicated the style – 01 for saison, 02 for session IPA and so on – then the second number was for the recipe they used. Dave and Tom tasted each and wrote down the results as they searched for the perfect recipe. Of course, the perfect recipe doesn't exist, so the numbers are getting pretty high. While many breweries

THE LOWDOWN

FOUNDED
2013.

ORIGINS
THE HOMEBREWING ADVENTURES OF TWO BELGIAN BEER LOVERS.

BRILLIANT BECAUSE
THEY ENJOY EXPERIMENTATION AND PUSHING THE BOUNDARIES OF TRADITIONAL BEER STYLES.

FLAGSHIP BEER
THEIR SAISON – OR STYLE 01 AS THEY KNOW IT – WAS THE BEDROCK ON WHICH THEY BUILT THE BREWERY AND IS STILL ONE OF THE BEST EXAMPLES IN THE UK. THEIR HOUSE YEAST GIVES IT PLENTY OF SPICE AND FRUIT SKIN AROMAS, BUT THE BEERS ARE ALWAYS LIGHT AND REFRESHING, JUST AS THE ORIGINAL BELGIAN STYLE WOULD HAVE BEEN WHEN IT WAS GIVEN TO SEASONAL FIELD WORKERS IN SUMMER.

SOUTH LONDON • Brew by Numbers

WHERE THE BREWER DRINKS

CHRIS AND TOM LOVE DRINKING AT THE DUKE'S HEAD WITH THE WELL-CARED FOR CASK ALES, OR AT MASON & CO, FOR THE SHEER BREADTH OF BRITISH BEER.

concentrate on 'dialling in' their core recipes, Brew by Numbers keep on starting from scratch. They live to play around.

'A lot of our beers are influenced by the science,' says Chris Hall, events manager and famous beer blogger himself. 'One of the biggest problems brewers have is that we do something twice and start calling it tradition. We should be changing things so they can evolve into what they need to be. In a couple of years the technology and processes will have moved on, and so will our beer.'

The beers Brew by Numbers are having the most fun with at the time of writing are East Coast IPAs – beers with a huge tropical fruit aroma and very low bitterness. They are one of the few breweries to adopt this style in the UK, and they make the best examples of it. The incredible aromas come from dry-hopping very early and not filtering, so it also means you end up with a completely opaque beer. Until recently, clarity has always been the sign of a well-made beer.

'We're going against the appearance of beer that has been built up for decades by commercial brewing,' says Tom.' When we first did that style, a few people were like "there must be something wrong with it". It's a bit of a backwards revolution, because all beer would have looked like it a hundred years ago.'

For such a scientific brewery, Brew By Numbers also like to take their hands off the wheel a lot too. While homebrewing, Tom and Dave had great success brewing saison, a dry, spicy blond ale from Belgium. These beers are yeast-driven, and yeast usually does exactly what it wants to, brewer be damned. But with care and attention to time and temperature, Brew By Numbers have come to produce a stunning British variety. It's now the beer the brewers drink the most, and the style that got the brewery on its feet in 2013.

'The London scene was pretty small back then,' says Tom. 'A brewery would get in a certain yeast strain and they'd collaborate or share it with another. One time a brewer got a French saison yeast and I think Brodies, Beavertown and maybe The Kernel used it at some point. By the time we got it it was several generations in and had mutated into something slightly different. But that sort of inspired us and we played around with it – we use pretty much the same one today. We love the versatility of yeast and will always experiment with it.'

The next step for the brewery is mixed fermentation – including wild yeasts found in the air or on fruit skins. It's some of the most difficult brewing you can do – with a lot of science in the run-up and a lot of chance in the aftermath. But as you walk around, tripping over bins labelled Wheely Dan and Wheely Nelson, you get the sense that they have the skills and the approach to nail it. Despite the claims that craft beer is for hipsters, really the brewing scene is a collection of engineers and scientists who happen to be really into flavour. There is very little pretence, but they take their beer very seriously indeed. It's a good motto to live by – take what you drink seriously and everything else seems more fun.

109

THE KERNEL

EXPORT STOUT
LONDON 1890

THE KERNEL

THEKERNELBREWERY.COM

THE BREWERY THAT STARTED IT ALL, KERNEL HAS SEEN
NEARLY 100 BREWERIES RUSH TO OPEN IN ITS WAKE, BUT IT
HAS QUIETLY CONTINUED TO MAKE SOME OF THE BEST BEER
IN THE COUNTRY AND IS REVERED THE WORLD OVER.

Ask any modern brewer in London why they went into brewing and at some point they'll mention The Kernel. Evin O'Riordain's quiet, considered influence is seen in every archway and trading estate brewery, tasted in every pale ale made inside the M25, and felt in every pub.

'I take no responsibility!' he cries when I imply as much. It's true it was never his intention, but Evin's brewery is where London's craft revolution started and he still leads it in his own way.

The Kernel doesn't make a lot of noise – the branding is simple and unchanging, their website gives very little away, and they even closed their taproom when it became too busy. But behind thick, damp walls they are doing some of the most important artisan brewing in the UK.

Suitably, the brewery vessels are hidden at the back of Evin's cavernous archway. Past his modest bottling line, a corridor suddenly opens up into a great chasm.

The brew house sits in the corner while the fermenters stand to attention on your left, dominating the room. Looking at the clipboards that hang from them is always enlightening. The Kernel is famous for never brewing the same beer twice, instead using different hops and regimes every time. Some might say it is being contrary, but the reason is simpler.

'All of us here take turns brewing and everyone has their slightly different approach. The hops change every time because the brewer changes every time. You'll see some brewers try to find hops that complement each other, while some will go the opposite and try to contrast them. When I brew I tend to go single hop – I like the simplicity of one hop telling you what it is.'

> **WHERE THE BREWER DRINKS**
>
> EVIN RECOMMENDS THE FOX ON KINGSLAND ROAD FOR THE BEER, OR CAFE OTO, DALSTON, FOR THE MUSIC AND THE BEER.

FOUNDED

2010.

ORIGINS

THE AWARD-WINNING HOMEBREWS OF FOUNDER EVIN O'RIORDAIN.

BRILLIANT BECAUSE

THEY BASICALLY STARTED THE WHOLE REVOLUTION, AND ARE THE MOST STAUNCHLY INDEPENDENT ARTISAN BREWERY IN LONDON.

FLAGSHIP BEER

I COULD WRITE SONNETS ABOUT KERNEL IPAS AND PALE ALES, BUT THE EXPORT INDIA PORTER EVIN'S BEEN MAKING SINCE HIS HOMEBREW DAYS DESCRIBES WHO EVIN IS BEST. MADE TO A RECIPE MORE THAN 150 YEARS OLD BUT HOPPED LIKE A MODERN IPA, THE DARK SWEET MALTS MINGLE WITH CITRUS AND PINE TO MAKE A LIQUORICE AROMA. THE BODY IS BITTERSWEET AND HEAVY WITH COFFEE. IT'S DECIDEDLY MODERN BUT ROOTED IN BRITISH TRADITION.

It's strange to hear Evin talk of simplicity given how complex his beers seem at first, none more so than the barrel-aged sours he is less famous for but just as skilled at. To find those you have to go even deeper into the Bermondsey abyss.

Despite the endless trains that rumble overhead on their approach to London Bridge station, stood in the barrel room you feel hundreds of miles from anywhere. This place has never known sunlight, and you can feel it. The darkness is complete, the air unmoving, and the temperature constant whatever the weather on the surface. Time seems to stand still, but inside the barrels everything is changing. Saisons are slowly turning lemony in Burgundy barrels, a stout is bubbling away as brett yeast does its work, and damsons are imbuing a

blend with intense red colours and flavours. It's magical how much life has been breathed into this dead space.

From these two caverns come some of my favourite ever beers. The IPAs are murky and laden with heady hop oils that make your brain swim; the Export Porter is all liquorice and toast with a kick of citrus; and the citra saison is dry and funky with heaps of grapefruit juiciness. The damson beer we tried while shooting was like cranberry juice – dry and tannic, but loaded with sweetness and funk to the point of near-Parmesan maturity. You can see Evin's eyes light up when he tries it, which makes sense when you know his background.

'My previous employment was selling cheese. One day my company asked me to go over to New York to help a customer set up a cheese shop. I'd be spending

all day teaching them "this is this cheese, it's made to this style, this is the animal and this is what they were eating and why the weather was important". After work those guys would take me out for a drink and tell me the same things about beer. They had the same relationship with beer that I had with cheese. I'd been drinking beer all my life and never made that connection. Well, there are certain things where once you're exposed to them you can't go back.'

Returning to London meant a return to boring brown bitters and flavourless lagers. Unable to find them appealing any more, Evin started making his own, eventually joining the London Amateur Brewers club, which held meetings above The Wenlock Arms in Islington. There he met like-minded people, many of whom went into brewing themselves. It was this sense of community that convinced Evin he could bring American brewing culture to the UK.

'To find that there were other people out there; people willing to take that risk, was great. There's a lot to be said for being in the right place at the right time – when we started there were nine breweries in London, but there were enough people who had had that American beer experience. I never felt any resistance.'

Some say that Evin's work has been fundamental to the creation of that community – there are now over 90 breweries in London – but he doesn't feel like the leader. Instead he takes the same approach he takes to his brewing: get the ingredients right, then let nature and time do the rest.

GIPSY HILL

GIPSYHILLBREW.COM

A TRUE TAIL OF RAGS TO RICHES, GIPSY HILL HAS GONE
FROM BLIND AMBITION TO BREWING SOME OF THE UK'S
BEST SESSION BEERS ON BOTH CASK AND KEG – AND THEIR
NEW EXPERIMENTAL BEERS ARE MAKING WAVES TOO.

Gipsy Hill Brewing Company nearly ended up in Spain. Founder Sam McMeekin had been plotting a craft brewery in his wife's homeland years before he met co-founder Charlie Shaw through a mutual friend. Charlie also had literal pipedreams about owning a brewery, and had taken a part-time job brewing and cleaning at East London's Five Points. It only took a few beer-fuelled meetings for Sam to scrap his plans and instead settle on a site near Crystal Palace. One of those meetings was spent force-carbonating an amber ale through an old keg, and that hatchet job became Southpaw, the first Gipsy Hill beer. Brewed by Charlie at Five Points in a spare fermenter, he admits it wasn't what he intended.

'Strictly speaking it wasn't supposed to be an amber,' says Charlie. 'It just came out too dark so I fully expected it to be awful. But it was actually really nice, so we called it Amber Magic and, once we got the keys to our brewery, the first thing that went in was 40 casks of that, which we sold to local pubs.'

The feeling that they might have ridden their luck made them put an advert out for a full-time brewer, and he came in the unique shape of Simon Wood. Long-haired and bearded with what he describes as 'a slight tramp vibe', Simon set about brewing the kind of sessionable but hoppy cask beers he'd been making down in the West Country.

'Simon replied to a very generic advert in Indeed.com or something that I'm not even sure we placed, but he was just brimming with enthusiasm,' says Sam. 'Plus when you're setting up a brewery you need someone with at least some kind of engineering background. He had that as well as years of brewing experience. Simon basically did everything from the brewing side right from the start.'

From these modest beginnings they have built one of the most forward-thinking and exciting breweries.

While Beatnik and Southpaw are delicious beers, they weren't much of a departure from the modern

cask ales being made all over the country by 2014. It was the addition of more experimental beers that gave the brewery momentum and put them on the path they're on now. Their session IPA, Hepcat, is just 4.5% but carries the body and flavour of a significantly bigger beer, with lots of overripe mango and passion fruit on the nose and a refreshing bittersweet finish. If that sounds good, how about their Yuzu fruit ale – all zingy citrus peel and coconut – or 2016's Bogan, a cloudy New Zealand pale ale hopped with Nelson Sauvin for a Juicy Fruit aroma, tempered by gooseberry and Chardonnay grapes. It was one of the best beers ever made in the UK.

What separates Gipsy Hill from many other breweries of their size is how focused their flavours are. It comes from their obsession with making tiny tweaks to their kit and their processes using what they've learnt from these experimental beers. There are hundreds, maybe thousands of touch points where a brewery can improve their beer – fermentation temperatures, hop timing, water chemistry – and more than any brewery I know, Gipsy Hill identify them and improve with every batch.

'Everyone has an obsession. For me it was craft brewing and looking at every angle and entry point,' says Sam. 'It's very different to the cask ales Simon was making before, so the learning journey he went on we all went on really. We come together to research techniques and all the time we tweak to get more out of the ingredients we're using. If anything that's accelerated now, but it was the story of the first year and a half when it was just the three of us.'

The brewery is now a hive of activity, not just on a Saturday when they open their doors to drinkers, but during the week when you can't hear yourself for the sounds of kettles boiling, bottles being filled,

THE LOWDOWN

FOUNDED
2014.

ORIGINS
THE DREAM OF TWO BEER LOVERS, BROUGHT TOGETHER BY A MUTUAL FRIEND AT A PARTY.

BRILLIANT BECAUSE
EVERY BATCH IS BETTER THAN THE LAST. THE CRAFT AND THE OBSESSION OF THE BREWERS ARE TANGIBLE IN EVERY PINT AND THE FLAVOURS THEY FIND ARE INCREDIBLE.

FLAGSHIP BEER
HEPCAT MIGHT NOT BE THE BEER THEY WOULD CHOOSE, BUT IT IS PERHAPS THE BEST SESSION IPA BEING MADE IN THE COUNTRY, PERFECTLY BRIDGING THE TWO MOST IMPORTANT SIDES OF GOOD BREWING – DRINKABILITY WITH A FULL FLAVOUR.

WHERE THE BREWER DRINKS
CONVENIENTLY THEY DRINK IN THEIR OWN BAR, THE DOUGLAS FIR. ORIGINALLY JUST A POP-UP (SIMON STRIPPED OUT THE OLD HAIRDRESSERS AND BUILT THE BAR HIMSELF), IT'S NOW A MICROPUB SERVING THEIR BEERS AND A FEW OF THEIR FRIENDS' BREWS. OTHERWISE YOU'LL FIND THEM MAKING A NUISANCE OF THEMSELVES AT WESTOW HOUSE DOWN THE ROAD FROM THE BREWERY.

fermenters being cleaned and some bearded guy welding in the corner. They now employ a small army and are forever growing.

Even with that growth, it's the same three people on the logo, faceless and unassuming. But one day, everyone who loves beer will know exactly who they are.

PUB SNACKS

**DRINKING RESPONSIBLY IS A MUST IN THE CRAFT BEER WORLD.
THE AVERAGE ABV OF BEER IS RISING FAST, AND ENJOYING A FEW
ON AN EMPTY STOMACH IS A ONE-WAY TICKET TO HANGOVER TOWN.**

———

Thankfully, British pub snacks have been through the same sort of revolution that craft beer has and nothing soaks up alcohol like British cuisine. So it follows that London is home to some of the best pub snacks in the world. We've come a long way since Nobby's nuts, but at least six of the seven pubs claiming to make 'the best Scotch eggs in London' must be lying.

My favourite is the pork bap from the Southampton Arms – a crusty, doughy bap filled with soft roasted meat, crispy crackling and sweet apple sauce, it's dynamite with the real ciders on pump or a malty red ale. Add a crossword and you've got my perfect Sunday.

The Stag in Hampstead genuinely does a mean Scotch egg, while The Kings Arms and Mother Kelly's do great meat and cheese platters. We should also never forget The Wenlock's sausage Sundays.

If you really need to line your stomach, The King & Co, The Duke's Head and The Rose & Crown all offer quarterly kitchens to street-food vendors; the Mall Tavern does great pies; Howling Hops some delicious barbecue; and Mason & Co has teamed up with Capish, who make hearty Italian-American food.

While some moan about the rise of food in pubs detracting from the convivial atmosphere, the combination is natural. It goes beyond sustenance – food and beer matches can be revelatory. IPA and mature Cheddar, stout and oysters, hoppy reds and burgers, Kriek and dark chocolate…these things were born to go together so why should we keep them apart?

FOURPURE

FOURPURE.COM

UNTIL RECENTLY FOURPURE WERE SEEN AS A LITTLE DULL
AND SERVICEABLE, BUT A FOCUS ON QUALITY INGREDIENTS
AND THE BEST TECHNOLOGY MIXED WITH SOME
NEWFOUND DARING HAS REVITALISED THE BREWERY.

At the start of 2016, Fourpure did a rebrand. When they founded four years before, craft beer was going through a strange phase. Like a kid in his dad's shoes several sizes too big, the industry was trying to look more grown up than it was. Fourpure's original branding was the embodiment of that. Sleek and clean, conceived by committee and completed by agency.

Founded by brothers Dan and Tom Lowe, the brewery takes its inspiration from their travels around the world. They made Bohemian lagers, West Coast IPAs and London stouts. It was exciting and forward-thinking, particularly the decision to can the beers long before it became the trendy thing to do. Cool as the cans were though, the branding didn't suit the beers

– outside it was all business, but inside was delicious craft chaos. I remember the first time I drank the IPA – crammed full of Christmas pine, sweet resin and citrusy bite. It was wild compared to the packaging.

Then craft beer cottoned on, and the brands making a name for themselves didn't take themselves seriously at all. They made absurd-sounding beers, with completely unmarketable names, and used ingredients you had never even dreamed of. They relished their place on the fringes of drinking culture and dragged people out to meet them. Fourpure was in danger of being left alone in the middle and they knew it.

The 2016 rebrand has been magic, transforming their look with eye-catching graphics that explain in just a

125

WHERE THE BREWER DRINKS
THE WHOLE TEAM LOVE THE KING'S ARMS IN BETHNAL GREEN FOR THE 'GREAT
SELECTION OF BEERS AND ABUNDANCE OF BEER HEADS TO TALK TO'.

few strokes what the beer and the brewery is about. But more than that, it's been part of a shake-up throughout the small company to respond to the movement away from the middle ground. Employing more experimental brewers to push recipes further has given the brewery a new lease of life. It's clear to see on the vibrant, exciting tallboy cans of Juicebox, a single hop IPA made with the zest of all sorts of citrus fruits. It's pithy and juicy but balanced and sinkable. It's an awesome summer beer, born for lazy afternoons playing French cricket or slowly getting frazzled in a festival field.

Now Fourpure finds itself in an enviable position. Hailed as one of the most important breweries for getting drinkers interested in good beer, they're also the kind of brewery that can cause a stir at a beer festival and create lines of people eager to try their latest seasonal. It's also led to collaborations with the trendiest breweries around the world, from Manchester's Cloudwater to California's Bear Republic.

As founder Tom Lowe says, 'We have always released one-off brews but they never made it much further than the taproom. We made a conscious

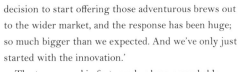

decision to start offering those adventurous brews out to the wider market, and the response has been huge; so much bigger than we expected. And we've only just started with the innovation.'

The turnaround in fortunes has been remarkable. Situated right on the edge of the Bermondsey Beer Mile, some of us wondered whether the brewery might fall off the map entirely. Instead, the taproom is at capacity even when London is grey and tries its hardest to piss on everyone's parade. We've witnessed drinkers determined to finish the mile clutch at cold pints under umbrellas – in fact, we've been those people. A small, gritty corner of Southwark has become a destination to drinkers all over the globe. Fourpure was formed when two beer lovers travelled the world; now it comes to them.

THE LOWDOWN

FOUNDED
2013.

ORIGINS
FOUNDED BY BROTHERS TOM AND DAN LOWE, FOURPURE WAS INSPIRED BY THEIR TRAVELS, WHICH JUST HAPPENED TO BE TO THE HOMES OF GREAT BEER – PLACES LIKE CALIFORNIA AND BAVARIA. THE NAME COMES FROM THEIR FOCUS ON RESPECTING TRADITIONAL BREWING METHODS AND THE FOUR INGREDIENTS INVOLVED.

FLAGSHIP BEER
FOURPURE WAS THE FIRST UK CRAFT BREWERY TO MAKE A GREAT LAGER, AND ARE STILL PERHAPS THE BEST AT IT. MADE WITH THE NOBLE CZECH HOP SAAZ, A HOP USED IN ALL THE BEST BOHEMIAN LAGERS, IT HAS A GORGEOUS SPICY AROMA WITH JUST A LITTLE LEMON, BALANCED BY THE BREADY MALTS. TO SOMEONE WHO HAS ONLY BEEN DRINKING MASS-PRODUCED LAGERS, IT WILL BE A REVELATION.

EAST

LONDON

EAST LONDON IS LIKE A NEON-LIT KEBAB SHOP. WE ALL DERIDE IT, BUT EVERY NOW AND THEN YOU FIND YOURSELF THERE, DRUNK WITH A BIG GRIN ON YOUR FACE.

No quarter of London has been through the change that the East End has. From industrial docklands through the swinging sixties and the Kray twins, to the recent invasion of media types, the change is accelerating.

That's not to say east London has lost its edge. Any night in a trendy bar can take a deliciously dark turn when you wander down the wrong alleyway and find yourself in a scene from *Luther*. New culture grinds against the rougher part, giving the area its character, especially in the pubs and breweries.

Picking five bars from the wealth of amazing drinking holes in Shoreditch, Dalston, Mile End and Hackney Wick is no easy task. The fact that property prices have only rocketed in the last two decades means there are plenty of freehouses, family-owned for generations and more likely to be free of tie. Where bars out west are broadly the same, variation in east London is the rule.

Take The Palm Tree, for example. Standing proud on the canal, it looks like the first building of a terrace that was never finished. Ghostly and rundown, I wouldn't blame you for taking one look and hightailing it to the nearest 'Spoons. Yet I find myself there regularly, even if the best thing you can say about the beer list is you'll get

a decent pint of Guinness. The place is full of character that has deserted most of London, and to me it is the very definition of that wrongly maligned term, the boozer.

The spirit of The Palm Tree endures in quite a few pubs in the East End. You could drink from a decent Belgian beer list in The Carpenter's Arms, once owned by the Kray twins, marvel at the faded glory of the Well & Bucket's glowing central bar and damaged walls, or try to spot the tiny Young Prince on Roman Road – a pub nearly two centuries old where I've heard tales the landlord used to get so drunk he fell over behind the bar.

None of these bars have the beer lists to make it into this book, but they do show that it's not just what you're drinking, but whom you're drinking with and where.

Nothing is more immersive than drinking beer in the brewery where it was made, and East London has two of the best brewery taps in the capital. In the factory heartland of Hackey Wick, Crate and Howling Hops have two glorious bars just metres from the fermenting tanks.

East London has perhaps the richest pub culture in England, and therefore the world. Now a glorious mix of the old and new, some East End pubs are almost as intoxicating as the beers we drink in them.

MASON & COMPANY

MASON & COMPANY

4 5 6

HOWLING HOPS BREWERY
AND TANK BAR

CRATE BREWERY
& PIZZERIA

MOTHER KELLY'S

MOTHERKELLYS.CO.UK

THE FIRST AMERICAN-STYLE TAPROOM IN LONDON, MOTHER KELLY'S HAS A WALL OF RARITIES IN THE FRIDGES AND 20 TAPS OF THE BEST CRAFT BEERS IN THE COUNTRY.

I've been 'lingering all alone down Paradise Row' many times, sat on Mother Kelly's doorstep. It's not just the pleasure I take from living out the lines of the song, it's that Mother Kelly's is one of the best bars in London. Inspired by the casual shop-like vibe of New York's craft beer bars, MKs is unlike the other pubs in this book. Set in a railway arch with floor-to-ceiling windows cutting it off from the outside, it's big, airy and bright. In a city where space is at a premium it's nice to not be bumping elbows with the drinker next to you. Instead you'll be in with the East End set, as this is the trendiest of the bars we've recommended. It has graffiti on the walls, uses absurdly shaped Teku taster glasses, and sometimes a dude rocks up and makes burgers in a smoker attached to the back of his motorcycle. It's the kind of effortless place that probably required a great deal of effort indeed.

My favourite time to visit is Saturday lunchtime, when you'll find the long sharing tables scattered with beer nerds, ploughing through cheese plates and having distracted discussions with their friends while eyeing up the beer fridge. The twenty taps usually have some remarkable things on, but it's this wall of beer that is most exciting. With five tall fridges, categorised from 'sour and lambic' to 'sharing bottles' via 'black-ish' and 'IPA', there is always something you have been dying to try. There are bottles in the fridges that you can't get anywhere else most of the year and they clearly travel themselves to get a lot of it. Belgians such as Cantillon and Hanssens usually need to be bought directly from the brewery, and the Scandinavian selection is usually exclusive to them.

The fridges may look great but they also serve a purpose. Beyond being best served chilled, beer needs to be kept at a constant, cool temperature to protect the precious hoppiness and slow the ruinous effects of oxygen. That means if a beer isn't in the fridge, it's probably spoiling. In the UK we store our beer on shelves and even in windows. In America, every good beer shop has its walls lined with fridges, keeping the

beers in the best possible condition. At Mother Kelly's, where it can get pretty warm on a Saturday night, keeping the beer constant is vital to how it will taste.

The fact that Mother Kelly's is central and more than a bit trendy means it plays an important role in the east London beer scene. There are lots of people coming in to drink who have no idea about beer. Faced with twenty taps and a few hundred bottles, that can be problematic.

While the bar caters to them with some more mainstream beers, as well as Prosecco on tap, it doesn't water down the offering. This has led to some glorious moments, such as when a group of builders who had just finished a job down the road found themselves drinking what I regard as the best lager (and maybe beer) in the world. Brought back from the giant, Bohemian forests of the Czech Republic just a few kegs at a time in the boot of a hatchback, it was ordered with a cursory 'six pints

of lager, please mate'. The men then set about getting very drunk without giving this seminal beer a moment's thought, save to say 'This is alright, isn't it?' Snobs may deride such an event, but for me it's a reminder of what beer should be. It may be artisan, challenging, a little overpriced and slightly full of itself, but when it comes down to drinking it, it's just a lot of fun. And that happens to sum up Mother Kelly's pretty well too.

BEERS	20 TAPS, GOD KNOWS HOW MANY BOTTLES. LOTS.
CULTURE	YOUNG, TRENDY AND LOUD IN THE EVENINGS, RELAXED AND VERY FRIENDLY BY DAY. A HOTBED FOR BEER-WRITER-SPOTTING, IF THAT'S YOUR KIND OF THING.

137

THE COCK TAVERN

PUB

THECOCKTAVERN.CO.UK

BRILLIANT BEER, PICKLED EGGS, CHEESE MOUNTAINS,
BEARDS. IF YOU LOVE ANY OF THOSE THINGS THEN THE COCK
TAVERN SHOULD BE YOUR GO-TO PUB IN EAST LONDON.

As the original and spiritual home of Howling Hops you'd expect the beer at The Cock Tavern to be good. What you might not expect is for its focus to be traditional real ale. When the brewery moved out east the location wasn't the only thing that changed – their beer mostly is in keg, but they still supply the old pub with cask ale, and here it is served exactly as it should be. There aren't many places in the capital that look after their cask as well as the Cock – perhaps it was because for many years they had a brewer in the next room to answer to. Twelve lines of fresh real ale and cider, pulled quickly from pumps to create big creamy heads and a tongue-tickling body. The beers are mostly from London, but if the beer is good they have no problem getting in something from Kent, Bristol and the heartlands of the north. The cask selection is staunchly British in its style though, with lots of bitters, stouts, scrumpy and even milds on. Hopheads have to go around the corner bar to the eight keg lines, whose chrome fonts stick out

against the burnished bronze cask pumps. There, the more modernist drinker can find plenty of Howling Hops, but also specials from the rest of London. They seem to have a particular love for Beavertown and Redemption, and who can blame them?

The varied and considered beer list draws a wonderfully mixed bag of locals. I've been in when at least four generations have been present, and with that comes a much more affable and easy atmosphere than you'd expect from a craft beer pub in the heart of trendy Hackney. I once left a scarf on a table, and had half the pub following me out to make sure it was returned safely.

As if being the former home of a bit of brewing history and still having one of the best tap lists of any pub in London wasn't enough, there is plenty more to keep you coming back. There's a beer 'garden' – and I only parenthesise because the pub does – that's just about passable in summer, and the bar snacks are commendable in lieu of a kitchen. There are five kinds

BEERS	EIGHT KEG AND TWELVE CASK LINES (AT LEAST FOUR GIVEN OVER TO CIDER), PLUS A SMALL FRIDGE OF PACKAGED LONDON-CENTRIC DELIGHTS. THERE ARE LOTS OF TRADITIONAL BEERS. DON'T EXPECT ANYTHING WILD OR COLLECTABLE, BUT FOR A NIGHT ON THE PINTS AND PACKETS OF CRISPS, NO PUB HAS A BETTER LIST.
CULTURE	ALL WALKS OF LIFE – OLD AND YOUNG, TRENDY AND NERDS, ALL RACES AND CREEDS. IT'S INDEFINABLE AND EXCITING. THE NIGHTS GET BUSY AND YOU'RE ALMOST FORCED TO MAKE FRIENDS, BUT IN A PUB LIKE THIS YOU'LL WANT TO.

of pickled egg on the bar (which must be some kind of record) and plenty of old-school crisps – a lot of fun can be had annoying the barman with samples while you try to find the perfect match. Time your visit right and you might witness the phenomenon they call the Holy Cheese Mountain, when a trolley is piled high with cheese for you to attempt to climb. Usually it's accompanied by a tap takeover from a brewer or cider producer so you can meet the makers while you drink and eat yourself to oblivion.

It may look dingy and gloomy from the outside; the 'CASH ONLY' and 'WATCH YOUR THINGS' may read like TURN BACK signs; the Nick Cave soundtrack may seem morose, but like all great pubs, The Cock Tavern feels like the kind of place you've been coming to for years from the moment you enter. The people, the speakeasy feel, the fact that the beer list seems to have been designed just for you make it feel like home. It's full of people who must have lived in Hackney way before it was cool and, like the pub, have nothing to prove.

If you are looking for the place that sums up London's entire beer culture, you'll find it in The Cock Tavern; and a lot more besides.

THE FOX

THEFOXE8.COM

ONE OF LONDON'S FIRST CRAFT BEER BARS AND STILL AMONG
THE BEST – A BUZZING ATMOSPHERE, FANTASTIC DRINKS
LIST AND EVEN A CRAFT BEER VENDING MACHINE MAKE IT
WORTH THE TRIP ALL THE WAY UP KINGSLAND ROAD.

You'll find The Fox at the exact point on the Kingsland Road where you start to think you've missed it. Gone are the halogen-lit Vietnamese cafés, the artisan chicken shops and trendy white-washed art galleries. The road widens and the traffic thins long before you see the rickety picnic tables that mark The Fox. The building has a looming, gothic quality to it, but inside the place is warm and excitable. It has a theatre-like feel with faded red sofas and a bar raised as if on a stage, where the taps become the set and the bar staff the actors.

But the real stars here are the beers, which have drawn people a mile up the Kingsland Road since the start of the revolution. If Evin of The Kernel chooses to drink beer at The Fox ahead of everywhere else in London, you know it's going to be something special. The beer list is incredible here, stretching across styles and continents with no real system other than being very discerning indeed. The bottle list alone is worth getting excited about – it can extend to 100, and is never less than 70. Hawaii's inventive and bold Maui beers have travelled halfway around the world to rub shoulders with Belgian classics like Westmalle, Australia's delicious Stone & Wood and the absolute best of British.

BEERS

ABOUT AS GOOD AS IT GETS AND WELL WORTH THE LESS-THAN-SCENIC WALK. TEN KEG AND EIGHT CASK LINES ALL KEPT WELL, TAKING IN ALL FOUR CORNERS OF THE GLOBE BUT BOUGHT WITH A DISCERNING EYE.

CULTURE

SURPRISINGLY UNBEERY GIVEN ITS REPUTATION. LOTS OF PEOPLE COME HERE FOR DINNER AND A FEW PINTS AFTER WORK ON A FRIDAY. IT'S THE KIND OF PLACE YOU CAN STAY ALL NIGHT THANKS TO THE GOOD FOOD AND BUZZ, WHICH MEAN NON-BEER DRINKERS WON'T ARGUE WITH YOU GETTING ANOTHER ROUND.

The pub is eternally buzzing, so the turnover on the kegs can be lightning fast. That means you never quite know what to expect. There's obviously a London bias but you'll also see hard-to-buy smaller breweries like old-school West Coast IPA lovers Odyssey, as much Cloudwater as they can get their hands on and Leed's awesome Northern Monk. On cask they keep it modern, sticking to hoppy numbers from Red Willow, Thornbridge and Tottenham's

Redemption. If the real ale is very modern, they haven't lost the traditional art of caring for it and it's one of the few pubs (next to The Southampton Arms and The Cock Tavern) where I might risk buying a pint without trying it first.

It's not just the beer that makes The Fox special, though. They make it feel like a true Public House with a full calendar of events and quirks like Wings Thursday (the name could be better, but the wings

probably couldn't), a photo booth I've never seen anyone use but heard everyone talk about, and even a craft beer vending machine. Quite why you wouldn't just go to the bar is beyond me but it's a very cool addition to posters, tin signs and bottles that adorn the walls.

It may be a trek but The Fox is one of the most loved and lauded craft beer pubs in London. A great way to break up the journey is to pub-crawl all the way up from Old Street, stopping at the Old Fountain, Electricity

Showrooms and Howl at the Moon before some restorative fried chicken at Chick'n'Sours or barbecue at the original Beavertown brewpub, Duke's. From there it's only minutes until you can fall through the door and demand the hoppiest, most bad-ass IPA on the menu. Pint in hand, you and your friends can lean on the raised bar, surveying the world of craft you have just conquered before crawling home via the mercifully close overground station.

MASON & COMPANY

PUB

MASONANDCOMPANY.CO.UK

COME SUMMER THERE IS NOTHING BETTER IN THE WORLD THAN
WATCHING THE SUNSET FROM A DECKCHAIR OUTSIDE MASON &
CO, A PINT IN ONE HAND AND MEATBALL SUB IN THE OTHER.

The best way to get to Mason & Co is to walk the canal. Normally I wouldn't recommend walking anywhere in London, but you need to approach the pub from a distance to get the full effect. Because as you walk along the water, breathing in the smoke from the wood burners of the barges, you wouldn't have any clue what kind of bar you are headed for. But then the big letters HERE EAST come into view, as do the huge cubist buildings of the former Olympic media centre.

Mason & Co is tucked into the front on the ground floor, its big windows looking out onto the water. From without and within there is something distinctly Scandinavian about the place. The minimalist décor, the exposed wood and flatpack Ikea furniture are totally out of keeping with the ideals of the owners, Five Points, and don't suit the American-Italian street food the kitchen serves, but it works perfectly in the big shell they inherited. What could have been a soulless pub feels like an airy temple to good beer.

It also gives them the space to fit in a few hundred people, as well as a giant bar with 20 taps and some solid beer fridges too. Strangely there is no cask, you'll find some of the best UK beers, from Verdant Brewing in Cornwall, to Lost and Grounded in Bristol, as well

147

BEERS

20 KEG LINES OF THE BEST BRITISH BEERS, WITH A FEW EXPORTS WHEN THE BEER BUYER IS FEELING EXOTIC. THREE LINES ARE ALWAYS FIVE POINTS, WHICH MEANS YOU'RE GUARANTEED A SOLID PALE ALE AND LAGER AT ANY POINT.

CULTURE

RAMMED IN THE SUMMER MONTHS, EMPTY ON A WINTERY MONDAY BUT A LOVELY PLACE TO BE ON EITHER OCCASION. THERE'S A MIX OF EAST LONDON TRENDIES, BEER NERDS FROM ALL OVER, AND A FAIR AMOUNT OF STUDENTS DODGING LECTURES AND ESSAYS.

as at least three taps of fresh Five Points. In the fridges things get even more exciting, with a vast array of rarer UK beers and a few imports. The beer list is good enough to drag people right from the other side of London, and out here it needs to be.

'It's true that it is a brand new destination. We originally started talking to the landlord about possible new premises for Five Points Brewery,' says Ed Mason, founder of the bar and the brewery. 'That didn't work out but they let us know about some bar and restaurant units they were fitting out. We loved the canal-side location and the massive outdoor area.'

That outside area is brilliant in summer, when you can take your pint out and spread luxuriously on the grass, watching the boats go by and pretending you're not in London. There's no need to crash back to reality any time soon either, because everything you need is right here. Mason & Co were the first to open on a short promenade of exciting independent retailers. Most notably there's a barcade (yes, that's a bar and an arcade in one) called Four Quarters, but there's also a decent wings shack and a modern Italian right next door. Not that you'll want to go anywhere with the incredible meatballs, subs and gelato coming out of the kitchen. While many pubs rotate their street food kitchens, the Italian-American chefs have a permanent home at Mason & Co, which means pretty much everyone leaves holding their stomach in but regretting nothing.

Those aren't the only draws either – there's an almost-weekly meet the brewer, usually out-of-towners to add to the draw. Cloudwater and Wylam came all the way down from the serious north for theirs, and that commitment only underlines how worth the trip Mason & Co is.

THE KINGS ARMS

PUB

WWW.THEKINGSARMSPUB.COM

IF THERE IS AN EXCITING BREWERY DOING A TAP TAKEOVER IN LONDON, YOU CAN ALMOST GUARANTEE IT WILL BE AT THIS UNDERSTATED EAST END BOOZER, WHERE AN EXCELLENT BEER LIST IS BALANCED BY EQUALLY GOOD CHEESE AND MEAT BOARDS TO KEEP YOU SOBER-ISH.

There's a Blogspot entry from early 2011 that describes The Kings Arms as 'by far the most traditional East End pub', boasting about Sky Sports and, seemingly, an illegal betting ring. Another enthuses that a pint of Foster's is just £2.90 and 'who can complain about that?' Perhaps a lot of people did, because since then everything has changed. In 2013 the old proprietors' family name 'Malindines' was scrubbed from the door and the pub given a complete overhaul. People may lament the fact they can't have a flutter on match days any more, but everything else is for the best.

Tucked behind the vibrant but grimy Bethnal Green Road you won't find any city suits or yuppy families at this bar. Even the thick-rim goggles of the beer geeks seem equally out of place at first. Where most pubs nail their craft colours to the mast, The Kings Arms hides them well. The long line of taps are unmarked; most punters walk straight past the rarities fridge on the way to the loo and the beer list on the wall looks more like a church hymn board.

But underneath its disguises, this pub takes beer very seriously indeed. If there's an exciting tap takeover happening in London, most bets would be on it happening at The Kings Arms. It's held Zwanze Day, Cantillon's hugely oversubscribed annual beer launch when pubs from all over the world crack a special keg at the same time. New York's Other Half, perhaps the best IPA brewery in America, threw some kegs on the bar one legendary night; and endlessly experimental Norwegians Lervig launched in the UK there. Even if you don't know the breweries it's worth going to an event at The Kings Arms, because their taste is impeccable.

When it's not hosting one of the world's best breweries, the pub still has sensational beer on across the keg and cask line-up. Between its 20 taps and

bomber bottle fridge you'll find beers you didn't even know made it to this country – from ultra-rare Mikkellers to world-famous mixed fermenters Jester King, all the way from Texas. It's the kind of place where a friend goes to the bar for a round and comes back with a pint each and a £20 sharing bottle because 'you don't see it in the UK very often'.

In fact, the fridge is what I love most about this pub. The rounds culture in the UK encourages us all to drink our own pints, sticking to what we know and not sharing the experience. But great beer is meant to be shared, and the bottle fridge at The Kings Arms encourages you to get a 750ml and four glasses to share and pour for each other. There is a connection in sharing beer and food that can't be replicated when nursing your own beers. It's certainly not the cheapest way to drink in a pub, but it does lead to the best nights and all kinds of delicious new discoveries.

Such a beer list demands sustenance, so in lieu of a kitchen the pub makes cheese and meat boards up

behind the bar with local produce and never quite enough crackers for the amount of topping they give you. I think it's all a ploy to make you stay and buy more. If it is, no one complains.

I bet there were mutinous mutterings when TVs were taken down and the Foster's tap ripped out. People probably raged about hipsters and gentrification in the heart of historic East London, but there is no doubt this is a better pub, a friendlier pub and a more legal local business. Also, for those who want a well-priced pint of lager, there's always Camden Hells on the bar for less than a fiver.

BEERS	FOURTEEN KEGS, SIX CASKS AND AN ABSOLUTELY OUTRAGEOUS BOTTLE AND CAN LIST THAT YOU COULD READ LIKE A NOVEL.
CULTURE	RELAXED AND CONVIVIAL EVEN WHEN IT'S RAMMED FOR AN EVENT. GET THERE EARLY, FIND A TABLE BY THE WINDOW AND WATCH AS IT FILLS UP.

CAMDEN TOWN	INK STOUT	4.4%	£4.5
EAVERTOWN	NECK OIL	4.3%	£4.
CHNEIDER EISSE	TAP 7 ORIGINAL	5.4%	£5.
LUSS	KELLERPILS	5%	£4.8
E KERNEL	PALE ALE	5.4%	£5.2
ITY	AMALGAMATION	8%	£6.C
ES	ANNIVERSARY #2	11.3%	£4.
RBLIOTEK	POP CORN HOP PORN	6%	£6.2

PINT	KEG	TO OL/ BUXTON	SKY MOUNTAIN SOUR
PINT	KEG	KEES	LVSTRO
PINT	CASK	MAGIC ROCK	DARK ARTS
PINT	CASK	PURITY	BUNNY HOP
PINT	CASK	DARK STAR	PARTRIDGE
PINT	CASK	MOOR	UNION'HOP
HALF	CIDER	MORTIMER'S	ORCHARD
PINT	CIDER	KENTISH PIP	VINTAGE

PUB GARDENS

THE PUB GARDEN IS A QUINTESSENTIALLY BRITISH THING. WE PROBABLY INVENTED THE PICNIC BENCH AND WHEN THE SUN ACTUALLY COMES WE'RE DAMN WELL GOING TO USE IT.

———

Sadly, space in London is at a premium and finding a pub with enough green space can be a challenge. Don't be fooled by the 'heated smoking area' or 'patio out back' – it usually means a gap no wider than a chimney shoot that fills up with a similar amount of smoke. Some do a little better: the Old Fountain has a lovely hidden roof terrace and at The Wenlock some take their pints across to Wenlock Park, though whether this is allowed is debatable.

Some of the best pub gardens aren't gardens at all. Crate, for example, is a wonderful place to drink by the canal but there isn't a hint of grass anywhere. Out west there are plenty of Fuller's pubs with terraces lining the Thames to make lovely watering holes, while down south the beer selection is a bit average, but the Duke of Edinburgh has a huge, buzzing garden.

It seems that the best places for golden hour are all in the north. The Stag in Hampstead has a brilliant garden, complete with another bar, can fridge and heated booths. Meanwhile, the nearby Garden Gate and The Spaniards Inn are special in the evening after hiking on the Heath, which is the best way to earn a pint in London.

HOWLING HOPS

HOWLINGHOPS.CO.UK

THE FIRST UK BREWPUB TO SERVE BEER STRAIGHT FROM THE BRIGHT TANKS, YOU CAN TASTE HOW FRESH AND VIBRANT THE BEERS ARE – AND THEY GO BRILLIANTLY WITH THE AUTHENTIC BARBECUE FOOD FROM THE KITCHENS.

If I could change one thing about people's beer-drinking habits, it would be to make them drink fresh beer. Decades of necking pasteurised, watered-down macrolager has led us to believe that freshness doesn't matter. We should treat it with more respect, and think of it like bread – it's best straight out of the oven and it gets slowly more stale from there. Oxygen, light and heat destroy hop aroma, distort yeast flavour and flatten malt body. Beer needs to be protected from them wherever possible, and for this reason the best beers you'll ever taste will be at the brewery itself.

At their brewpub in a cavernous Hackney Wick warehouse, Howling Hops take this a stage further. They serve their beer direct from the bright tanks, which line up behind the bar like soldiers ready for battle. The beers from these vessels have never seen light or oxygen, or been at room temperature. They've travelled a few metres through steel pipes before being poured to order and delivered straight to the drinker. Anyone could taste the difference.

THE LOWDOWN

FOUNDED
2011.

ORIGINS
THE BASEMENT OF THE COCK TAVERN BREWPUB, WHICH UNTIL 2015 WAS ITS HOME. HOWLING HOPS STILL STOCKS THE PUB, BUT MOST OF IT IS SOLD IN THE TAPROOM OR TO PUBS ALL OVER LONDON.

BRILLIANT BECAUSE
BY CHAMPIONING TANK-FRESH BEER HOWLING HOPS IS DOING THE WHOLE CRAFT BEER SECTOR A SERVICE, WHILE POURING SOME OF THE MOST VIBRANT AND EXCITING BEERS IN THE CAPITAL.

FLAGSHIP BEER
IT HAS TO BE THE BOHEMIAN PILSNER. UNLIKE ANY MACROLAGER OR EVEN THE MORE FULL-FLAVOURED CAMDEN HELLS, THANKS TO ITS GORGEOUS BUTTERY AROMA, TEMPERED BY NOTES OF LEMON AND STRAWBERRY.

THE U.K'S FIRST D

Take their Pilsner, a style known by most people as a tiresome beer sold for a pittance by supermarkets. But Howling Hops's is full-bodied, with notes of caramel, brown bread, lemon and even strawberries; it's a wild, delicious beer that jumps from the glass. If that's not craft enough for you, their IPA is like shoving your face in a bag of hops – all heady spice, tropical fruit and pithy bitterness. Even their low-abv tanks are full of big flavours, the 3.5% Running Beer is a citrus bomb that explodes like a beer twice its strength. The magic is in the brewhouse, but it's maintained by the way it's served.

'The biggest benefit of serving beer directly from the serving tanks is that the brewers can keep a keener eye on the product,' says head brewer Tim O'Rourke. 'We can adjust the temperature and carbonation level to match the style of the beer. For example, our Imperial Stout is served at about 10°C with fewer bubbles than the Pils at 5°C.'

It's a technique that has always worked for Howling Hops, which started in the basement of The Cock Tavern in Hackney Central. There they made keg and cask beers that were mostly served from the taps above. The freshly hopped beers brought crowds from all over town, but moving to a dedicated site with beer tanks has given the brewery an even better reputation.

'You get the freshest product possible, which is especially important for the low-ABV pale ales we tend to produce the most of. Nothing compares to that nearly harsh hop brightness you get off a beer that's only days old.'

The beers here feel alive and so do you when you drink them, hence why I usually head down there the day after the night before, when I need a pick-me-up. Saturday and

WHERE THE BREWER DRINKS

TIM LIKES TO DRINK AT HIS OLD HAUNT, THE COCK TAVERN IN HACKNEY, WHICH HE CALLS HIS 'SECOND HOME'.
THE PUB STILL STOCKS LOTS OF HOWLING HOPS NEXT TO SOME OF THE COUNTRY'S BEST CASK AND KEG BEER.

Sunday mornings in the taproom are as relaxed as a pub can get. Three wooden tables stretch the entire length of the renovated warehouse, and small groups of drinkers drape themselves across the benches. The beer comes in two-third mugs, and just the act of holding them can clear any cloudy heads. The unpasteurised beer inside them feels nourishing, full-flavoured and refreshing.

The food is exceptional too. Served from a hatch and paraded around the room until the barman finds the hungry customer, it only takes a few glistening burgers, platters of pulled pork and sweet potato chips the size of your pint to go by before you have to indulge. Happily,

it's easy to be trapped there for most of the day.

Come the evening things get significantly more rowdy. There's usually a DJ spinning vinyls and people dancing down the aisles. On West Ham United match days the place is overrun, and the chances of you getting a pint of their amazing lager are considerably diminished. But it is always good-natured, which I think comes down to the relaxing effect the place has. No one ever seems drunk or out of place. Whether it's standing room only or an empty Sunday session, everyone in that taproom is thinking the same thing: that beer should always taste like this, and pubs should always feel like this.

FIVE POINTS

FIVEPOINTSBREWING.CO.UK

**TAKING A VERY BRITISH APPROACH TO THE AMERICAN
HOP REVOLUTION, FIVE POINTS MAKE AN ULTRA-
DRINKABLE RANGE OF LAGERS, PALES AND IPAS AS
WELL AS SOME BRITISH-INSPIRED SEASONALS.**

Most craft brewers want to break from the past –
the dirge that we used to call beer and neck on Fridays
without really knowing there was an alternative.
You see it in the beers, the branding, the people and
the parties.

But some breweries don't seem so concerned with
that and there is a timeless feel to Five Points that can
only be matched by Fuller's in London. Of course, the
former is some 170 years younger, but their approach
recalls the golden ages of London brewing.

While some breweries were readying their bourbon
barrels and buying hop cannons, Five Points were
quietly dialling in their pale, red and porter recipes and
mostly casking them. You see, there are many ways to
innovate and Five Points chose a different route. They
were using 100% renewable energy, donating profits to
charity, becoming the first London brewery to pay the
Living Wage and setting up a brewery apprenticeship

scheme with the local college. They are a truly
grassroots business, stuck firm in the heart of Hackney
and refusing to budge. In that way, they've had plenty of
influence over the capital's brewing scene.

'When we opened we wanted to be embedded in
our local community,' says Ed Mason. 'I wanted a
social conscience and to run a business that isn't just
about the bottom line. Now there has been a move to
a neighbourhood brewery model, where almost every
borough has its own brewery that the locals get behind.'

Perhaps the inspiration came from running pubs
for most of his career, the kind of job that instils the
importance of the local in you. This more modest
approach to business stretches to the beer too. Ed's
friend Greg Hobbs was looking for a step-up from his
brewing job just as Ed had sold his pub, Mason & Taylor.
He used the money to set up the brewery, dealing with
the business side while Greg set about brewing.

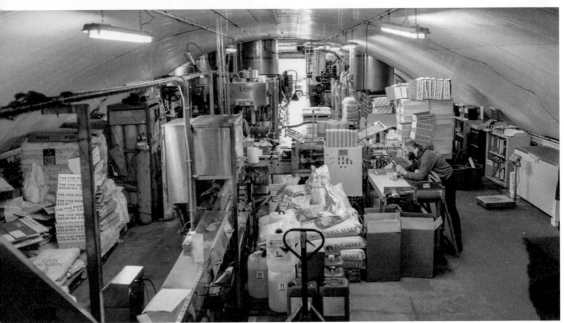

Greg had come from East London Brewing Company, a locally focused cask brewery, and took the opportunity to add some modern twists to his traditional roots. The Pale Ale, which makes up the majority of their production, uses British Maris Otter malt but American Citra and Amarillo for piney and pithy orange bitterness. Hook Island Red, which could also be described as a strong ale, has been made with tangy rye malt and big, bitter American hops. The Railway Porter is the most traditional, with dry chocolate and coffee notes, but also comes as a special spiked with brett yeast, cleverly named Derailed Porter. Those twists were designed to appeal to the new drinkers while remaining true to their vision of sessionable beer.

'We want people to take our beers to their hearts as their "go to" pale, or IPA or porter, and we want to reach out to as many people as possible. We are proud to produce flavoursome beers that are accessible to as wide an audience as possible.'

If that sounds like a dig at those who don't make accessible beer I can assure you it's not – for a start, Five Points got a barrel-ageing programme underway recently. It's more an acceptance of their place in the world of beer. For the craft breweries of the world to take the market back from the dull brewing practices of the macros, there has to be great beer for the majority. Beautiful, well-made pale ales and lagers that are brewed and enjoyed locally will be the beers that bring about the change.

Drinking local means getting the best flavours from your beer, but with Five Points it also feels like a lifestyle choice. When you have a cask of it at The Cock Tavern or the Old Fountain, it's with a feeling of pride at being part of something bigger than the pint you are holding.

WHERE THE BREWER DRINKS

THE AWESOME COCK TAVERN IS RIGHT AROUND THE CORNER FROM THE BREWERY, BUT YOU'RE MOST LIKELY TO SEE THE TEAM AT MASON & CO, WHICH IS OWNED BY ED.

THE LOWDOWN

FOUNDED
2012.

ORIGINS
THE LONG-TERM DREAM OF PUBLICAN ED MASON, WHICH CAME TRUE AFTER SELLING HIS MUCH-LOVED LONDON CRAFT BEER BAR MASON & TAYLOR AND TEAMING UP WITH FORMER EMPLOYEE AND ELB BREWER GREG HOBBS.

BRILLIANT BECAUSE
THEY MAKE CONSISTENTLY DELICIOUS FLAVOURFUL BEERS THAT YOU CAN DRINK ALL NIGHT. IT IS THE KIND OF BEER THAT, IN THE IDEAL WORLD, WILL BE ON THE BAR WHEREVER YOU GO.

FLAGSHIP BEER
THEIR PALE ALE MAKES UP TWO-THIRDS OF THEIR CAPACITY AND RIGHTLY SO. IT'S A MALTY BUT RASPINGLY BITTER BEER WITH LOTS OF PINE NEEDLES, ORANGE RIND AND JUST A LITTLE CARAMEL.

URBAN FARMHOUSE

REDCHURCH.BEER

EASILY THE MOST EXPERIMENTAL BREWERY IN LONDON, YOU WON'T
SEE MANY HOPS OR SHINY METAL TANKS AT URBAN FARMHOUSE –
THEY LOVE WILD YEASTS, FORAGED HERBS AND WOODEN BARRELS,
MAKING SOME OF THE MOST EXCITING SOUR BEER IN THE UK.

'At our first ever tasting we gave everyone Tartlette saying, "Just so you know, this is a very sour and unusual beer." Straight away a guy put his hand up and asked "How dare you ask someone to pay for this? It's revolting." Then he finished his glass and walked out.' Many would lose heart at such a review, but James Rylance took it as a good sign. It showed that his new approach was working.

James has been in the background of many of the great moments in modern London brewing. He started by brewing at The Kernel, then was in Logan's original team at Beavertown before joining as head brewer at Redchurch. When they expanded into a huge brewery out in Harlow, he was left with a rundown but very usable brewing site. Rather than move out, James saw the opportunity to make the space his own. Although Urban Farmhouse is associated with Redchurch, the only links are James and the building.

'I spent the first part of my career learning, and the next bit having an idea of what I wanted to do and not being able to do it. I learnt a lot at Kernel and Beavertown but now there's complete freedom. I get to do everything I've wanted to, and find my own frame of reference.'

By that he means a farmhouse brewery, but right in the heart of east London. 'Farmhouse beer' is a term bandied around but never really used correctly. In simple terms it means using the ingredients around you –

WHERE THE BREWER DRINKS

WILLIAM IV IN LEYTONSTONE IS OWNED BY BRODIE'S BREWERY AND SERVES A WIDE RANGE OF THEIR BEERS. IT'S ALSO KNOWN FOR ITS OAP JAZZ NIGHT, WHEN AGEING RETIREES COME TOGETHER TO PLAY JAZZ FOR THE ECLECTIC CROWD. JAMES LOVES THE BAND SO MUCH HE NAMED HIS BRETTANOMYCES YEAST AFTER THE 90-YEAR-OLD DRUMMER, CYRIL.

174

which historically would likely have been a farm. It's not just about the hops, grain and water – spicy or funky wild yeasts have become the defining characteristic of farmhouse beers, even if they are unique to each brewery.

Yeast is all around us. It collects on surfaces and fills the air, especially in old buildings such as Urban Farmhouse's railway arch. James was able to isolate and propagate his own strain of brettanomyces from the walls of the brewery and uses it as the basis for his beers. He blends that strain with other bacteria and yeasts to create local characteristics in his beers. These blends are cropped off one fermenting beer and siphoned into the next, giving all his ferments a telltale ciderous aroma and puckering sourness. That's the basis of James's farmhouse concept, but he takes it further.

'It's amazing what food grows inside the M25, and if it doesn't we get stuff from my parents' farm in Shropshire. So the vast majority of our beers have more herbs than hops. Some taste like they have been hit with loads and loads of American citrusy hops but nah, man, it's all herbs.'

One such beer is the delicious Life of Plants, a tart blonde beer made with lemon verbena, lemon thyme, bay and sage. The aroma is like traditional lemonade – powdered sherbert and sour lemon – but the bay and sage add savoury notes that dip in and out on the tongue. It is wild, savoury and sour, three words few people associate with brewing. You don't need to love or even appreciate beer to enjoy James's – he and his novice brewer Jack Dobbie, former manager of the awesome gastropub the Marksman, want to appeal to all lovers of flavour.

'Our backgrounds are in food – I was a chef before and Jack's birth was even announced on a specials board. When we took him on it was part of our attempt to get out of that brewing culture, or even the idea of brewers making beer. Everyone took the pale ale, IPA, stout model and ran with it but we've only lived off pale ale in the last few years. Brewing never used to be like that.'

It feels like while so many brewers are trying to wrestle back control over nature – dictating temperatures and disinfecting every surface they can see – James wants nature to take over his brewery. Like in the wild, there is a chaos to the brewery that only makes sense when you look very closely. The same goes for his beers – the aromas and flavours can overwhelm you at first, but as you break them down you realise they are perfectly placed.

'I think it was the beer writer Michael Jackson who said lager making is like a perfectly recorded studio album. Brewing like this is more like a live performance. There will be ups and downs and you might not be able to hear or understand bits, but it's chaotic and it's beautiful because of that.'

In the barrels and flat, squat fermenters of Urban Farmhouse are some of the UK's most live and challenging beers being made in London, unlike anything that's ever been made in London before, but now quite literally a taste of the East End.

CRATE

CRATEBREWERY.COM

THIS CANAL-SIDE BREWPUB OPENED IN 2012 AND HAS STRUGGLED TO KEEP UP WITH DEMAND EVER SINCE THANKS TO THEIR DELICIOUS SESSION BEERS AND PAPER-THIN CRISPY PIZZAS.

If you asked your average Londoner to name a craft beer bar, the chances are they'd say Crate. On one level it's because you could take your mother and she'd have a great time, but there is more depth to Crate than that. Located within keg-rolling distance of Stratford, they opened just in time for the 2012 Olympics. Within the year, the canal-side brewpub had escaped the craft beer bubble to go mainstream. If that makes it sound easy, director Neil Hinchley swears it wasn't.

'We'd been offered the White Building because Jess and Tom [co-founders] had a successful cafe nearby,' he says. 'We went to see it and were presented with a rat-infested former squat – before that it was used to print porn and counterfeit money. We inherited a renovated shell and decorated it with reclaimed material on a shoestring. I guess it's because we were kind of the first to do that, but it became an up-cycle Mecca. We were just doing it out of desperation!'

If the incredible use of space and old wood were a big draw, they were nothing compared to the crispy pizzas and fresh, modern beer. Crate topped every *Time Out*-style beer bar list produced, and was rewarded by more and more hungry and thirsty beer lovers. They were halcyon days of summer, spent watching the sunlight creep down the graffiti across the canal, drinking pints and making friends at the giant picnic tables. The start was so busy that the brewery was fit to burst and the chefs making the pizzas had to double the amount of dough they made every day.

But as demand grew, Crate seemed to lose its way. As the crowds gathered, the waiting times for pizzas topped an hour, and the service became strained. More worryingly, though, the quality of the beer dipped and there was even talk of batches not being brewed on site anymore.

The buzz around the beer faded and I stayed away for well over a year until a friend suggested meeting there for a pint, and out of curiosity I agreed. On the surface nothing had changed, but to my surprise I noticed a single-hop amarillo pale ale on tap. Even in its heyday Crate had not really invested in specials – capacity

WHERE THE BREWER DRINKS

NEIL 'FINDS HIMSELF' IN MOTHER KELLY'S QUITE A LOT BECAUSE OF THE BEER, WHILE CALUM LOVES STORMBIRD FOR THE CRAZY BEER RANGE AND MISMATCH FURNISHING.

wouldn't allow it – so I ordered two immediately. Fifteen minutes later my friend and I were still exclaiming about how good the beer was. Light and fluffy, just a little hazy and oozing with candied, orangey hops. It wasn't long before we were back at the bar ordering the other specials. We had a citra single hop – clean as a freshly chopped grapefruit – and a sweet and nutty American brown ale. Since then I've been back numerous times and found the pale beers rival those coming out of any other London brewery.

Neil has invested heavily in his brewhouse and team, who are bringing back seasonality to make sure their list constantly moves. They innovated in other ways too.

'Opinion is hard to change, so we started canning.

It was a big shift for us, but people don't notice the small differences,' says head brewer Calum Bennett. 'We started brewing complete different beers, as well as tweaking the core beer. We started doing interesting wild beer projects like ageing a beer on raspberries. That was really tasty so we've done another on blueberries. I'm sure something good will happen, but we don't know what it is!'

That sour raspberry ale, secondary fermented solely on the yeasts found on the fruits, is as good as Calum says. Light and fruity on the aroma, but with a deep, mature acidity that fills your mouth, nose and head with gorgeous scrumpy-like notes.

The brewery needed that year in the wilderness. In the fast-moving world of craft beer you have to keep progressing. Ingredients vary, palates change, drinkers move on. In 2018 the brewing side of Crate will have to move as the yard it sits on is redeveloped. They have big ambitions for the new brewery and it's safe to say they won't lose their way again.

180

THE LOWDOWN

FOUNDED
2012.

ORIGINS
FOUNDED BY FORMER FILMMAKER NEIL HINCHLEY WITH
SIBLINGS JESS AND TOM SEATON, WHO RAN THE COUNTER CAFÉ
DOWN THE ROAD.

BRILLIANT BECAUSE
THEY HAVE SCORED THEMSELVES ONE OF THE BEST LOCATIONS IN
LONDON, AND THERE AREN'T MANY BETTER PLACES TO ENJOY GREAT
PIZZA AND A PINT. THE BEER HAS COME ON IN LEAPS AND BOUNDS
AND WITH THEIR MIXED FERMENTATION MAKE THEM ONES TO WATCH.

FLAGSHIP BEER
THE CORE RANGE IS STILL VERY SAFE, SO GO STRAIGHT FOR
THE SINGLE-HOP PALE ALES. EVEN AT 4.5% THEY ARE FRUITY,
BITTERSWEET AND FULL-BODIED. THE MIXED FERMENTATION
BEERS ARE WORTH A TRY TOO, IF YOU'RE INTO WILD BEERS.

WEST

LONDON

LET'S BE HONEST. WHEN IT COMES TO BEER, WEST LONDON IS A DESERT.
A MAN IN SEARCH OF A DECENT DRINK CAN STAGGER FOR MILES OVER
DUSTY CONCRETE DUNES AND FIND NOTHING TO SLAKE HIS THIRST.
THERE ARE PLENTY OF MIRAGES – BEAUTIFUL OLD PUBS AND HISTORIC
INNS – BUT FEW OF THEM WILL STOCK ANYTHING OF ANY WORTH.

Cliché though it may be, the Notting Hills and Chelseas are more into Champagne and French reds. The big, whitewashed townhouses are more likely to house an embassy than a good, British beer pub. But there are oases spread across this arid land. Sometimes you don't realise until you are practically on top of them, while others scream out across the plains, 'Salvation is this way!'

If you can't find one of the amazing pubs in this section, or God forbid find yourself so deep into the desert that you might die of thirst before you reached one, West London does have one amazing redeeming beer feature – Fuller's.

Fuller's brewery is without doubt one of the most important British breweries, and indeed companies, still working today. From its home in Chiswick it still produces some of the best traditional real ale in the world, and its staunch defence of great beer has played no small part in the survival and revival of British beer. But on a more personal note, the brewery has saved me from thirst on many occasions when out West. You see, Fuller's also has a few pubs. And by a few pubs I mean a few hundred. In the SW postcode.

The 400 or so they claim to have seems a gross underestimate. You can't walk 50 metres in Hammersmith without winding up at the bar of a Fuller's pub (or at least I can't) and most of them are very good. Occasionally the beer selection is limited, and the food is often the identikit kind of 'pub grub' you'll find in some much less lovely establishments, but a fresh cask of ESB really cannot be beaten, and that alone makes a visit to this craft beer wasteland worth the visit.

But there are other very good beery reasons to give West London a go. It has one of the most exciting pub concepts in the country in the Italian Job, the capital's most underrated brewery in the shape of Weird Beard, and easily the best BrewDog bar in the UK. Know where you're going, and West London will make sure you survive your ostensibly beerless walkabout.

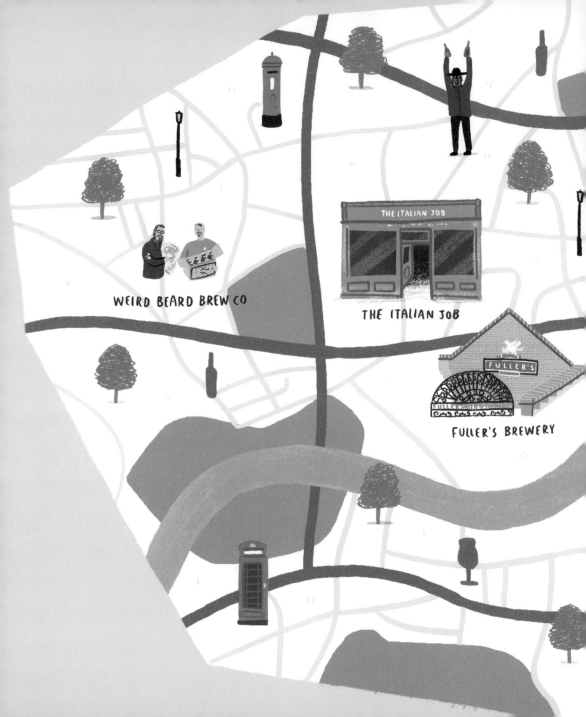

WEIRD BEARD BREW CO

THE ITALIAN JOB

FULLER'S BREWERY

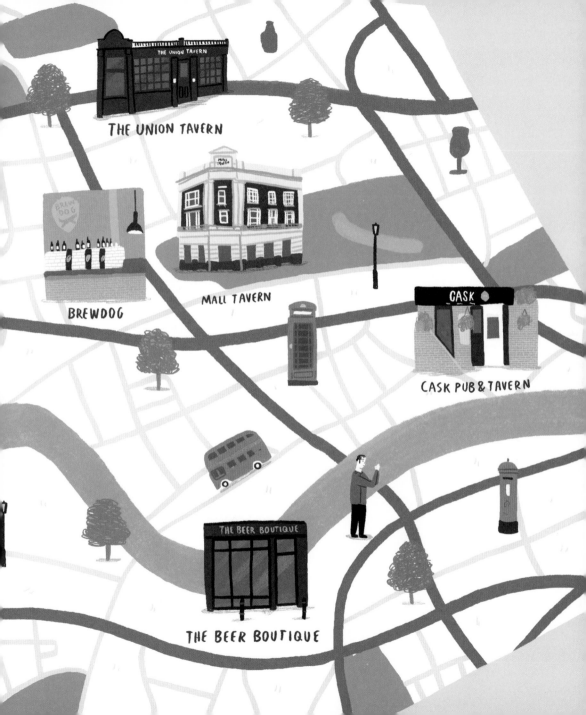

THE UNION TAVERN

BREWDOG

MALL TAVERN

CASK

CASK PUB & TAVERN

THE BEER BOUTIQUE

THE ITALIAN JOB

THEITALIANJOBPUB.CO.UK

NESTLED AMONG THE BOUTIQUE STORES AND MILLIONAIRE
MANSIONS, IT'S AN UNLIKELY PLACE FOR A BEER BAR,
BUT THE ITALIAN JOB IS WORTH SEEKING OUT FOR A
TASTE OF ITALIAN CRAFT AND CAFÉ CULTURE.

For a country that considers Tennent's Super a premium beer, the quality of Italian craft beer is incredible. Breweries like Birrificio Lambrate, Birrificio Italiano and LoverBeer produce some of Europe's best beers, none of which would make it to the UK if it weren't for a brilliant little bar in West London. The aptly named Italian Job is a joint venture between some moneyed beer lovers and arguably Italy's best modern brewery, Birraficio Del Ducato. Despite lots of business nous they chose the most bizarre place in London to start a craft beer bar, but thankfully the delicious beers and food have helped it thrive.

Found just off Chiswick High Road, deep into the washed white desert of West London, the bar is almost indistinguishable from the boutique stores that also line the street – have a few too many here and you might find yourself weighed down by designer handbags and silk scarves by the time you hit Turnham Green Tube.

Inside is a very different story. Exposed brick, ironwork and retro light bulbs (that shed almost no light at all) are more reminiscent of Shoreditch. It's remarkably warm for the industrial look though, which might be down to the cosy dimensions – 10 square tables are all they can fit.

As expected, most of the beers are from Del Ducato but they make a wonderful, varied array of beer. The ever-present smoked amber lager is a joy – kind of like candied bacon – and the IPA claims to be a West Coaster but is far too smooth and drinkable, despite the waves and waves of citrus. They keep the list moving too, with saisons, stouts, double IPAs (try Machete, you only need one glass) and even a California common, an almost-extinct, slightly tart copper ale. Perhaps these breweries are so experimental because Tennent's is so big in Italy, not despite it. Andrea Neri Galanti, who runs the Italian Job, certainly thinks so. 'Italian craft beer is a young scene born out of the necessity of

artisans and beer lover to express their concept of beer,' he enthuses. 'It's the result of the love, creativity and passion of amazing people who have put together their knowledge and cultural heritage to brew devotedly and uncontrollably.'

Andrea is full of Italian verve – all arms and high speed talk as he bustles about the bar and takes people through the selection. His staff are some of the most attentive in London too. If you ask for a new beer, they always ask you to try it first. Perhaps that's a symptom

of being in a part of town not acquainted with sour, smoked or even hoppy beer, but I think all pubs should take note.

Of course, it rarely applies to me because I want to try everything, and I recommend you do too. This pub is a window to a whole new brewing culture, accessible without even leaving London, and it's worth taking the time to make sure you get the best of it. Once you're done with the draught, there is more variation in the fridges, with plenty from other breweries. There seems to be even more eclecticism in Italian brewing than British – all kinds of flavours, bottle shapes, branding and styles.

'The Italian craft brewing scene started in 1996 and since then the number of microbreweries has surpassed 900. We do not have a tradition to follow; no new creation we come up with is going to disdain our ancestors, and we never feel like we have to wrestle with an ancient tradition to come out on top.'

Whenever I go to the Italian Job I am overcome with envy. Head to a British-themed bar abroad and you'll be confronted with Foster's taps, manky carpets and, probably, mostly British clientele. At the Italian Job the staff are Italian but the patrons are all Brits escaping the identikit Chiswick High Street. The pub is both rooted in its Italian origins while totally transcending them to become a fantastic British beer bar. Just like the first craft brewers in the UK, Del Ducato have found a niche no one really knew existed.

BEERS	EIGHT KEG AND TWO CASK LINES OF MOSTLY DEL DUCATO BEERS, WITH THE ODD GUEST. IN THE TWO BIG FRIDGES YOU'LL FIND LOTS OF ITALIAN BREWERS TO KEEP YOU GOING IF YOU'VE EXHAUSTED THE DRAUGHT.
CULTURE	A SLIGHTLY OLDER CROWD AND QUITE A FEW DATES. DON'T COME WITH A BIG GROUP OF FRIENDS – THIS PLACE AND THE BEERS ARE GREAT FOR QUIET NIGHTS CATCHING UP WITH FRIENDS, WHO PROBABLY NEED TO BE BEER LOVERS.

BREWDOG SHEPHERD'S BUSH

PUB

BREWDOG.COM/BARS/UK/SHEPHERDS-BUSH

BY FAR BREWDOG'S BEST LONDON BAR, WITH EVERYTHING THAT MAKES THEIR SITES GREAT – ENDLESS IPAS, AMERICAN FAST FOOD AND RETRO ARCADE GAMES.

Since brewing their first commercial beer together back in 2007, James Watt and Martin Dickie of BrewDog have made a lot of noise. At various points they have taken swings at everyone from UK alcohol advisory boards all the way up to Vladimir Putin.

All the while they have been producing stunning beers that paved the way for others. There have been lots of gimmicks and stunts, but all have been in the pursuit of levelling the playing field in an increasingly monopolised brewing industry. Founded in Fraserburgh, an isolated town north of Aberdeen, their influence is now felt all over the world thanks to their chain of bars. BrewDogs can be found everywhere from Norwich to Tokyo, via Sao Paolo and Helsinki. Interest is so keen that a fake one even sprung up in Hong Kong. True, there's irony in the fact that brewery-owned pubs were one of the scourges of good beer in this country,

and yet the fiercest rebel against that system now owns over 50 itself. Seen as exploitative and self-serving, brewery pub estates often only serve their own beers and a centrally controlled food menu of frozen pies.

But that's not always the case. Whether you love or loathe BrewDog, it's impossible for a beer geek to have a bad time at BrewDog Shepherd's Bush. This huge bar has forty taps with nearly half given over to other craft breweries, as well as a massive fridge selection that groans under the weight of fantastic indie beer from around the world.

It is a brewery pub done right, and that means there are some very obvious benefits. Their internal distribution means the beers are arriving fresh and well cared for, and it's a great opportunity to try all their beers in the best condition they can be outside of the brewery. I've had some tired Punk IPA in my time

BREWDOG DRAFT

PUNK IPA
LIVE DEAD PONY CLUB
DEAD PONY CLUB
5AM SAINT
JET BLACK HEART
VAGABOND PALE ALE (GF)
KINGPIN LAGER CANS
BLITZ
ELVIS JUICE
TRASHY BLONDE
HELLA HELLES
NANNY STATE BOTTLES
CHILI HAMMER
ELECTRIC

PROTO RED ALE 4.5% £5.65

BEATNIK IMPERIAL RED 8% £6.50½ -SHAREHOLDER EXCLUSIVE

ELVIS JUICE 6.5% £5.50⅔

HELLA HELLES 4.7% £5.20

LAUNCHING TONIGHT AT 6PM!! - ACE OF EQUINOX 4.5% £5.15

GUEST DRAFT

KERNEL IMPERIAL BROWN STOUT 9.5% £4.10½

BEAVERTOWN BLACK BETTY 7.2% £4.55⅔

WEIHENSTEPHAN FESTBIER 5.8% £5.35

BEAVERTOWN LUPULOID IPA 6.7% £5.50⅔

GREEN FLASH WEST COAST IPA 8.1% £4·35½

STONE BERLIN CALI·BELGIQUE 6.9%£5.55⅔

MIKKELLER ICH BIN CHERRY 3.7% £3.50½

FLYING DOG BERLINER WEISSE 4.2% £4.90½

BEAVERTOWN GAMMA RAY 5.4% £5.80

WIFI· welovebeer

.%£·

KERNEL TABLE BEER 2.8% £5.20

KERNEL BIERE DE SAISON CITRA 4.6% £5.10⅔

LINDEMANS FRAMBOISE 2.5% £4.00½

BEAVERTOWN HOLY COWBELL 5.6% £5.45

FIERCE BEER BLACK FLAGSHIP 6.5% £4.10⅔

WEIRD BEARD SMOKE 5.1% £5.95

SIREN PROTEUS V4 APOLLO BRAVO SIMCOE 4% £5.80

PRESSUREDROP PALE FIRE 4.8%£4.55⅓

SIREN LIQUID MISTRESS 5.8%£4.80⅔

WEIRD BEARD FIRE 5.1% £5.95

BUXTON **X** OMNIPOLLO LEMON MERINGUE ICE CREAM PIE 6% £5.55⅔

BREWGOODER LAGER 4.5% £5.20

STONE BERLIN GO TO IPA 4.7% £6.40

CREW

but on draught at Shepherd's Bush, the bright, zingy grapefruit is there in spades. You'll also be able to try some of the smaller-batch experimental beers, usually launched at 6pm on a Friday – great seasonal brews like Elvis Juice, Electric India and, my favourite, Born To Die, a hugely fruity IPA that's thrown out if it's not drunk within 90 days. The variety on show here is baffling and you can spend a whole night there drinking different beers without ever leaving the BrewDog canon.

For all the bold beers and showy marketing, as a BrewDog site Shepherd's Bush is actually very understated. The tiny sign outside is completely lost in the distressed metal, and the floor to ceiling windows give them little room for 'motivational' messages or

'hop propaganda', as they would call it. There are still some awesome neon signs though, which add to the American feel they've brought to the bar with the big fridges, high stools, retro arcade games and pinball machines. That US influence reaches the food too, which is all burgers, wings and dogs served in tacky plastic baskets, called things like Cluck Norris and The Patriot Burger.

It may not be as punk as the founders would have you believe, in fact it's about as punk as Johnny Rotten in a butter advert, but it is a fantastic bar serving fresh beer from one of the UK's best craft brewers, and if that means filling this book with Hop Propaganda, then so be it.

BEERS — FORTY KEG LINES AND ONE 'LIVE BEER' LINE, PLUS BEERS FROM ALL OVER THE WORLD IN THE FRIDGES.

CULTURE — VERY QUIET DURING THE DAY, WITH A PARTY ATMOSPHERE AT NIGHT.

THE MALL TAVERN

PUB

THEMALLW8.COM

A HISTORIC TAVERN THAT SERVES AS A BEER OASIS IN NOTTING HILL, THIS FANTASTIC PUB HAS A HUGE BEER MENU AS WELL AS A CHEF'S TABLE, BEER CELLAR AND LIBRARY ROOM TO EXPLORE.

On the tills at The Mall Tavern there's a button labelled 'Betty'. Pressed at least three times a week, it's a sign of the kind of place the pub is. It's there for one local, a 93-year-old called Betty, who met her husband here decades ago when they shared a sad afternoon off work in the aftermath of an IRA bombing in the 1970s. Now widowed, Betty comes in frequently for lunch. One day she admitted that she wanted to come more, but she refused to pay more than £10 for a meal. The staff agreed she could have anything on the menu for £10 as long as she came in three times a week. Sure, there was a financial benefit, but it was mostly because Betty tells excellent stories. The Betty button was born so the tills could process her discount.

'I mean there's a straight shot of humanity right there,' enthuses the pub's owner, Jonathan Perritt. 'You have people with ugly beards like mine and Betty in the same room, a West London millionaire hammering her £10 meal deal while the rest of us pay £7 a pint for an Evil Twin or something. That's what pubs are about.'

The fascinating history of Notting Hill, which saw huge immigration and race riots followed by quick gentrification from the eighties onwards, means this is a diverse part of town. Pub culture definitely suffered as a result of it all though. Owned by giant companies, most were slow to adapt to the constant changes around them. The Mall has managed to embrace it all.

'You have to accept that the heartland of British brewing isn't in West London, and when we went free of tie and spoke to one or two of the new breweries – the

BEERS	SIXTEEN KEG OF MOSTLY NEW-WAVE BRITISH CRAFT BEER WITH MORE TRADITIONAL BEER ON CASK AND ADVENTUROUS STUFF IN THE FRIDGES.
CULTURE	CERTAINLY OLDER THAN THE CRAFT PUBS OF EAST LONDON, BUT DISCERNING, LIVELY AND OCCASIONALLY RAUCOUS. QUITE A SLOW STARTER, SO IF YOU GET IN EARLY THERE IS ALWAYS A SEAT.

ALES & CIDERS

Beavertowns and such – they weren't even delivering to this part of town. But these days people know what they're drinking and if they're spending over £5 a pint, it needs to be excellent. Luckily we had a relationship with those breweries through our other site at the time, and that helped persuade them.'

And the beer list is indeed excellent. The ever-changing line-up of 16 kegs is always carefully chosen, and if a few more cask lines would have been nice you still know it's well cared for. As well as a focus on southern UK craft brewers, they seem to have a great love of canned beer and rarer American imports like Two Roads and Evil Twin. All this means you're guaranteed to try something new every time you go in.

You could also end up in a totally new room, because the pub is labyrinthine. Aside from the bar which fits over 100 people, there's a beer cellar complete with antique wooden doors, five more taps and a wall lined with beer cages, gently ageing or awaiting their turn in the bar fridges. Upstairs there's a library room, which looks like the set from a bad BBC whodunnit, as well as a chef's table. Inspired by the sought-after tables of Michelin-star restaurants, guests can sit in the heart of the kitchen watching the food being prepared and getting served by the chefs themselves. You can tell the chefs relish the opportunity to play host and amazingly the table is booked most nights.

In a part of town not associated with good pubs, Notting Hill is very lucky to have The Mall Tavern. They've had to adapt to survive, filling a giant space with life and soul, teasing out the bits of history and updating the other parts. You know you are in a special place when someone like Betty keeps coming back, year after year, as everything outside changes. It's not just the best pub in West London, it might be one of the best pubs in the capital.

CASK

CASKPUBANDKITCHEN.COM

IT MAY FEEL LIKE A 1980S CONSERVATIVE CLUB, BUT ONE LOOK AT THE AMAZING DRAUGHT SELECTION AND JAW-DROPPING LAMBIC FRIDGE SHOWS THESE GUYS KNOW HOW TO PUT A BEER LIST TOGETHER.

In a part of London famous for its squares and Regency architecture, Cask has just about the most inauspicious location you can find in Pimlico. Nestled into a 1960s ex-council block it looks more like a cornershop than a pub, and inside it feels like they just knocked through a few flats to make room.

Cask, though, happens to be one of the original London craft beer pubs. Founded in 2009 it was miles ahead of other trailblazers and in terms of its cask and bottle list it still is. It's also the first site of the Craft Beer Co estate, which now has bars across London. Evidently Cask wasn't a cool enough name so that had to go, but otherwise they are all very similar, including the slight Conservative Men's Club feel inside.

What they lack in taste for interior design they more than make up for in the beer. The 25 taps are all killer, no filler. Their house lager is a world beater in the delicious Rothaus Pils – big, bitter and bready – and it's upwards from there with lots of carefully chosen independent breweries from all over. They have no bias to style or region, stretching from London to Cornwall, then over the ocean to America with the likes of Founders and Sierra Nevada (never the core stuff, always the specials).

But it's on cask where Cask, unsurprisingly, comes into its own. Ten pumps of British real ale, all

BEERS

FIFTEEN KEG AND TEN CASK, AS WELL AS AROUND 100 BOTTLES, ALL EXPERTLY CHOSEN AND CARED FOR. PRICES CAN BE HIGH BUT YOU KNOW IT'S GOING TO BE DELICIOUS.

CULTURE

HALF OF THE PEOPLE FIT IN WELL WITH THE WEIRD MEN'S CLUB VIBE, WHILE THE OTHER HALF ARE STUDENTS, TOURISTS AND BEER NERDS SO YOU NEVER QUITE KNOW WHAT TO EXPECT WHEN YOU GO IN. THE LIVE BLUEGRASS MUSIC ON A SUNDAY JUST ADDS TO THE INTRIGUE.

CASK TARIFF
UP
TO >3% = £3.85
4% = £4.15
5% = £4.35
6% = £4.65
7% = £5.35

CASK

CHINOOK
SORACHI

BLACKJACK
SPECIALS
Snake Hunt

WEST LONDON • Cask

perfectly kept, take up half the bar. Keeping the beer flowing is key to keeping your beers fresh, and no barrel seems to stick around long. They even have a board by the bar telling you what's conditioning in the cellar and will be on the pumps soon. If it's to be believed they have a lot of casks to look after down there and throughput must be very fast indeed. There are plenty from the smaller cask breweries around the country, people like Gun and Vibrant Forest who rarely get to the capital except in a package. These more backwoods breweries make hazy, unrefined ale full of character – the kind of beers London brewers rave about but are rarely seen on the bar. Any pub that seeks these beers out deserves your patronage.

The same thought and exploration goes into their bottle list, which for some wonderful reason is very heavy on the lambic and American bombers. With one-third off all takeaway beer you can make quite the haul of tiny Belgian farmhouse sour beers. Tilquin and Hanssens make up the majority, even including Hanssens' Strawberry lambic, of which there can only be a few thousand bottles made each year. American sharers come from all over, with lots of the Bruery and Almanac which have come all the way from the West Coast. You get the feeling the range is so good because everyone comes here to drink cask, but that means if you're lucky the lambics will have a bit of age on them, which the majority need to really develop in the bottle.

A hardcore beer nerd could spend hundreds here on beer he has never tried, but the joy of Cask is that his friends will be equally happy with the selection. To be honest, in this part of town you'd be happy with anything that isn't Heineken, and that makes the effort that has gone into Cask all the more commendable.

THE UNION TAVERN

UNION-TAVERN.CO.UK

A FULLER'S PUB WITH A DIFFERENCE, SERVING A CAREFULLY
CURATED SELECTION OF LONDON BREWERIES NEXT TO THEIR
OWN TRADITIONAL CASK BEERS. THE OLD WORLD MEETS NEW,
WITH A CANAL-SIDE BEER GARDEN THROWN INTO THE MIX.

The Union Tavern is another Fuller's pub, but it's been modernised in all the ways an ageing loafer-wearer would do it – barbecue food, quirky blackboard messages and a keg wall that shouts 'trendy' but the cask lines and older clientele give the game away.

If that sounds derogatory, it's not meant to. For a start, those CAMRA bods will put a pint away before you've even had a sniff of your beer. But also, The Union Tavern has found its own kind of cool and the beer selection can be really, really good. It is focused exclusively on London, which is a brave move even with 100 breweries at your disposal. You put yourself at the mercy of the latest trends – which seems to be American pale ales whatever the season – but they try to mix it up. It also makes sense to buy in bulk, so you'll find one brewery each week seems to dominate, whether it's Crate or Beavertown or Fuller's itself. When they get the chance, though, they aren't afraid to put a sour Berliner Weisse or gose on tap, which opens up the more exploratory brewers in the

capital like Brew By Numbers and Urban Farmhouse. Fuller's may be seen as a slightly fusty company, but there is nothing conservative about the beers on keg.

It's not just the beer list that's surprising. The Union Tavern has plenty hidden depth, quite literally as it goes across two floors and it's not immediately obvious how to go down or up. On the lower level it has a canal-side beer garden to rival Crate's, though with a very sensible railing, as well as a good whisky selection and American barbecue food, all smoked in-house. They could go much bigger on all three assets but perhaps that's where the owners have drawn the line.

There was no line drawn in the bathroom though. There's a fantastic painting on the walls of the men's loo, depicting a the Fuller's griffin stood on the deck of a sinking ship as a lamb (the logo of Young's) jumps off. It's an allusion to how Young's stopped brewing in the capital back in the dark days of 2006, while Fuller's stayed true to their roots. It's surprisingly combative but

then former head brewer, John Keeling, revels in that kind of humour and the brewery has been proved right by not abandoning ship or compromising.

The Union Tavern – hell, even Fuller's itself – could have easily become middle of the road and boring. Instead it serves great, adventurous beer to absolutely everyone in a location crying out for better pubs. What's more, it can only get better as the London brewing scene comes of age. In fact, The Union Tavern's 12 London keg lines are proof it might have already.

BEERS	EXCLUSIVELY LONDON BREWERIES (THOUGH SOME SUBURBS LIKE WINDSOR DO SNEAK IN) ACROSS THE FIVE CASK AND 12 KEG LINES, WITH A HEAVY FOCUS ON THE OWNERS, FULLER'S.
CULTURE	COME EARLY AND IT WILL BE LIKE ATTENDING A CAMRA MEETING, COME LATER IN THE WEEK AND THE YOUNGSTERS TAKE OVER. AT THE WEEKEND, IT'S THE CLASSIC FIGHT FOR TABLES AMONG THE PRAMS AND GIN DRINKERS, BUT THAT MEANS MORE BEER FOR US.

LADIES
UPSTAIRS

BOTTLESHOPS

**THE CRAFT BREWING REVOLUTION HAS GIVEN RISE TO ALL SORTS
OF NEW AND UNEXPECTED BUSINESSES – CRAFT MALTSTERS,
HOMEBREW SUPPLIERS, BEER SOMMELIERS. BUT THE MOST
OBVIOUS DEVELOPMENT HAS BEEN THE BOTTLESHOP.**

———

The first ones were just forward-thinking off licences like Drinkers Paradise in Kentish Town, who bought in some of the new local beer as well as some more famous American imports. Nowadays they are like mini beer supermarkets with rows upon rows of craft bottles and cans, homebrew equipment and merchandise. Some even have 'growler stations' where you can fill flagons with fresh draught beer to take home. If that sounds like heaven, it's because it is.

Only Hop, Burns & Black has made it into this book, by virtue of its amazing beer selection and the fact you can have a crafty beer while you shop, but there are hundreds of bottleshops throughout London now – Caps and Taps, Clapton Craft, We Brought Beer, Kris Wines, Utobeer, Kill the Cat, Bottle Apostle and Pig's Ears, on top of some great off licences that look like nothing from the outside.

It's a risky business to try to compete with Tesco Express, but bottleshops have saved us from dire supermarket BOGOFF deals, so you should support your local bottleshop whenever you can.

FULLER'S

FULLERS.CO.UK

AS THE LONGEST-LIVING FAMILY BREWERY IN LONDON, FULLER'S IS A BEACON OF HOPE IN A BUSINESS DOMINATED BY MACROLAGERS AND SUITED ACCOUNTANTS. BY KEEPING ITS TRADITIONS BUT LEARNING FROM THE NEW MOVEMENT, FULLER'S SHOULD BE AROUND FOR CENTURIES TO COME.

It's strange to think that in 100 years we might talk about Beavertown or Kernel the way that we do about Fuller's. It is the capital's oldest living brewery, still mashing in every morning near its original site in Chiswick. In its 150-year life, Fuller's has been through a lot that might have finished off other breweries – the invention of pasteurisation, two World Wars, the proliferation of keg beer and the near extinction of real ale. And yet it still stands, just miles away from where others have fallen, still loved by beer drinkers the world over.

Bizarrely, this rich history and critical acclaim means that some don't think of Fuller's as a craft brewery. Of course, it depends on your definition, but I think a family-owned cask-focused brewery has as sound a claim to craftsmanship as any modern brewery. Where some see a fading grandparent in their West London retirement home, others see a feisty veteran, still full of life and tales to tell.

Fuller's have made some decent attempts at brewing the modern, hop-forward styles championed by the new guard, but it's not where their head or heart is at. Since the first pint of Chiswick was poured in the 1930s, Fuller's has been king of the British bitter.

This style is pretty much ignored by young London drinkers, and it's their loss. When on form, a classic bitter is as richly flavoured and complex as any IPA. The only difference is the flavours don't come from the hops. A good bitter balances the yeasty esters of banana, pear and clove with the raisin or caramel sweetness of the malt. I don't need to tell you how good that beer sounds, and what I am describing is effectively Fuller's ESB. If a cask of this beer is kept well and poured right, it is a revelation. All fruitcake on the aroma and dark caramel on the tongue, before a residual juiciness from the yeast gives it a long, aromatic finish. Drinking a

WHERE THE BREWER DRINKS

JOHN CONSIDERS DRINKING 'A MOVEABLE FEAST' BUT HE MOSTLY DRINKS AT FULLER'S OWN BELL & CROWN, RIGHT ON THE RIVER NEAR RICHMOND.

FOUNDED

1845.

ORIGINS

THE BREWERY WAS CREATED IN THE 1600S WHEN CHISWICK LOCAL THOMAS MAWSON INHERITED A SMALL COTTAGE BREWHOUSE ON CHISWICK MALL. HE BOUGHT UP ANOTHER ONE AT BEDFORD HOUSE, AS WELL AS THE LOCAL PUB AND TWO MORE COTTAGES. THE BREWERY CHANGED HANDS A FEW TIMES (GAINING THE NAME OF THE GRIFFIN BREWERY AFTER WHICH THE LOGO WAS DESIGNED) AND EVENTUALLY CAME TO JOHN FULLER, WHO WAS BROUGHT IN TO SAVE IT FROM FINANCIAL RUIN. MORE INVESTMENT CAME FROM A FELLOW BREWERY OWNER, JOHN SMITH, WHO INVESTED ON BEHALF OF HIS SON HENRY AND SON-IN-LAW JOHN TURNER. HENCE FULLER'S, SMITH & TURNER WAS BORN.

FLAGSHIP BEER

LONDON PRIDE. FIRST BREWED IN THE 1950S IT HAS COME TO DEFINE WHAT A BRITISH BITTER TASTES LIKE – RICH, SMOOTH AND FRUITY WITH JUST A HINT OF BITTERNESS FROM THE KENT HOPS. THE BREWERS THEMSELVES SEEM TO LOVE THE ORIGINAL CHISWICK BITTER THOUGH.

fresh ESB or Chiswick Bitter in a Fuller's pub by the Thames should be on everyone's bucket list.

But Fuller's don't just make bitters. They've been barrel ageing big beers since 2008, and each year release their Vintage Ale, made to a slightly different recipe every year and designed to be stored. You can buy yourself a bottle of the first edition from 1997 for an almighty £515 on the brewery's webshop and enjoy the fantastic marmalade and tequila-oakiness the beer picks up. Their imperial stout is also worth buying by

the case to age. Being nearly 200 years old gives you the perspective and patience you need to create beers that take time to come into their own.

The man behind these forays into experimental beers is now-retired John Keeling, who had been head brewer at Fuller's for decades and worked there since finishing his degree in brewing at Heriot-Watt. He's seen the decline of British beer and its dramatic rebirth, and takes great pride in being part of the new movement. In the days before the brewing renaissance, London Pride and ESB dominated the cask pumps all over the capital. Given that modern brewers working in the capital grew up drinking these, Fuller's has perhaps had the greatest influence on the London beer scene of any brewery.

'We were craft before the term was invented and have always had this great interest in flavour, which is the core of craft brewing,' says John. 'In fact, you don't get more craft than to invent a beer style as we did with ESB way back in 1979! However, I think it is more two-way than that and we have things to learn from the new kids on the block too. Their enthusiasm and ability to think outside the accepted ways of doing things is inspiring to any brewer worth his salt.'

The rise of all these small breweries could have been a threat to a traditional brewer like Fuller's. But in a revolution mostly seen in the keg lines, British cask is having a revival too. Real ale has flavours no other form of dispense really can, thanks to the unique way it is kept and served. It is a vital part of our brewing history for sure, but it is also a vibrant part of its future.

'British cask is unique – nowhere else in the world produces cask in such quantities; no other beers successfully marry this low carbonation, serving temperature and flavour; nowhere else can you go to the pub and experience this remarkable beer in all its glory.' In Fuller's, London has been blessed with great beer.

217

FULLER'S HOCK CELLAR

BREWED BESIDE THE THAMES SINCE 1845

FULLERS

1952 · 1977

SILVER CELEBRATION

Extra Strong Bitter

Brewed & Bottled by Fuller Smith & Turner Ltd
"Griffin Brewery Chiswick England

FULLERS

Strong Ale

275 ml 9.68 fl oz

FULLER SMITH & TURNER LTD CHISWICK
BREWED IN ENGLAND

WEIRD BEARD

WEIRDBEARDBREWCO.COM

BASED IN AN INDUSTRIAL PARK WELL OUTSIDE WHAT CAN LEGITIMATELY BE CALLED CENTRAL LONDON, WEIRD BEARD HAVE NEVER FOLLOWED THE CROWD. IN FACT, THE BEARDS ARE PROBABLY THE LEAST WEIRD THING ABOUT THE BREWERY.

To say that Bryan Spooner lives and breathes his own brand would be an understatement. He is the embodiment of the brewery, from his foot-long beard to the skull tattoo on his neck, and he looks like he was born in his overalls.

He'd been homebrewing and winning awards for a few years when he became disillusioned with his job and started looking to go pro. Responding to a tweet about a brewery business opportunity, he went and met some other homebrewers to discuss teaming up.

'There were a few of us involved to various extents and I remember it felt like all we were doing was talking,' he says. 'I got frustrated and spent some time on my nightshift working on a name and a logo. I presented what I had to them all, saying "I'm starting a brewery called Weird Beard Brew Co, here's the logo. Who's with me?" Only Gregg and myself went forward.'

Gregg Irwin, who happily sported a goatee himself, became Bryan's business partner, sorting the legalities of the new brewery while Bryan saw out his notice. They found a site out in Hanwell in 2013, bursting onto the scene with skull-laden branding and brash beers. They quickly made a name for themselves with their dank, hoppy IPAs and full-on dark beers like Black Perle, a coffee milk stout. They had a subtler side too, brewing a 2.8% dark mild with the second runnings of their imperial stout and a hoppy table beer called Little Things That Kill. In the first few years they produced an astonishing variety of beers, as if they were still looking for something. As well as endless IPA variations they added a canned lager, Faceless Spreadsheet Ninja, and an imperial bitter called Boring Brown Beer, on top of saisons, American wheats, smoked beers, dark lagers, red ales and more. Very little of it stuck though.

FOUNDED

2013.

ORIGINS

GREGG AND BRYAN WERE TWO AWARD-WINNING HOMEBREWERS, BROUGHT TOGETHER BY A TWEET, NO LESS. AFTER WEEKS OF TALKING ABOUT MAYBE STARTING A BREWERY, THEY FINALLY GOT THINGS TOGETHER WHEN BRYAN SHOWED GREGG A SKETCH OF THE BREWERY LOGO. GREGG HAS SINCE LEFT THE BUSINESS, BUT IT'S STILL GOING STRONG.

BRILLIANT BECAUSE

THEY MAKE ALL THE KINDS OF BEERS NO ONE ELSE WOULD MAKE. MODERN MILDS, SINGLE HOP SORACHI IPAS, CRANBERRY CHRISTMAS STOUTS AND MORE.

FLAGSHIP BEER

MARIANA TRENCH; ON ITS DAY, IT IS ONE OF THE BEST PALE ALES IN THE COUNTRY, WITH LOADS OF CITRUSY AMERICAN HOPS BUT SOME RIOTOUS BITTERNESS AND SPICE FROM THE PACIFIC GEM.

'We would all hate just brewing the same five or so beers all the time,' explains Bryan. 'Yes, there is a challenge getting core beers as consistent as possible, but that will soon get boring. We want to push ourselves; we want to experiment. It is a huge part of what we are.'

That's not to say they don't have a core range though. Every brewery needs a beer it's known for, one that defines who the brewers are. For Weird Beard it's Mariana Trench, a complex American pale ale that uses hops from the US and New Zealand for a citrusy

and spicy aroma. Every time I drink it I pick out a new flavour profile – from pepper to mango – not something you can say about every core American pale ale.

You'd think the short attention span might hold the brewery back, but they now have three warehouses to fit all their brewing, beer and people in. That's a luxury they wouldn't have if they'd put themselves in the crowded arches of Bermondsey or Hackney. It has also pushed them to create some of the greatest beers London has produced. For example, their insane Sorachi Faceplant is just about as exciting

as a hoppy beer can get and sums up Weird Beard's approach to brewing. It uses the Japanese hop Sorachi Ace, giving this giant IPA the aroma of bubblegum, sherbet-lemons and even coconut. It's the kind of hop most brewers would use with extreme caution but Bryan and his crew throw tons of it in the fermenters whenever they get the chance.

Weird Beard defiantly go their own way, and it has made them one of the most underrated London breweries. For me there are few more exciting sights at the bar than a Weird Beard beer you have never heard of.

WHERE THE BREWER DRINKS
BRYAN'S FAVOURITE PUB IS THE DODO IN EALING, WHICH HAS BECOME THE BREWERY'S UNOFFICIAL TAPROOM AND THE BEST PLACE TO TRY THEIR BEERS FRESH ON CASK.

CENTRAL

LONDON

CENTRAL LONDON. THE VERY PHRASE CAN BRING SHUDDERS TO A BEER
LOVER'S SPINE. HOME OF THE CHAIN PUB, SERVING A SEA OF LAGERS TO
AN OCEAN OF SUITED AND BOOTED PERONI DRINKERS. WHEN I THINK OF A
CENTRAL LONDON PUB I PICTURE PEOPLE SPILLING OUT THE DOOR WITH
PLASTIC CUPS, E-CIGARETTES AND RESIGNED LOOKS ON THEIR FACES.

The problem with having a pub in a WC postcode is that
you don't feel like you need to try. You can make your
volumes and margins pouring beer that would make a
true brewer blush. The pubs are always busy thanks to
the roaring tourist trade, then when 5pm comes around
the offices spill out and the bars get even more crowded.
How do pubs get away with serving bad beer? To be
honest, with the queues at the bar some people are glad
to get served at all.

But if you know where you are headed, you can avoid
bad beer and soulless, faceless bars. In fact, there are
plenty of good places to drink in the West End and
slightly to the east – there are some fantastic pubs we had
to leave out in favour of other, even better ones. Take The
Holborn Whippet, for example, serving lovely local craft
beer and pizza right by Holborn Circus; or BrewDog
Soho, closer to Oxford Circus than any other craft beer
chain could ever hope to be; and the Old Coffee House,
proudly serving exclusively Brodie's beer. There's even

Temple Brewhouse down by the river, serving cask beer
made on-site and a collection of other breweries' beers.

All these pubs are refuges from the wilderness of
Soho beer culture, but none of them quite compete with
the fantastic shortlist of pubs available to those within
the Congestion Charge zone. The Harp is the kind of
place that tourists imagine when they think of a British
pub – cosy, eccentric and dominated by real ale. There is
also a true beer institution in Lowlander, a Belgian beer
bar that has been slaking the thirst of stranded beer
lovers since 2002. Further away down Old Street, where
East London meets the City you'll find two of the best
pubs in London, let alone WC.

It's a sign of how far craft beer has come that you
can now drink locally made, exciting and unusual beers
within sight of the Royal Opera House or Regent Street.
Good beer has become as much a part of London as
the Thames and delays on the Piccadilly line, but it is
considerably better than both.

THE EXMOUTH ARMS

LOWLANDER GRAND CAFE

THE HARP

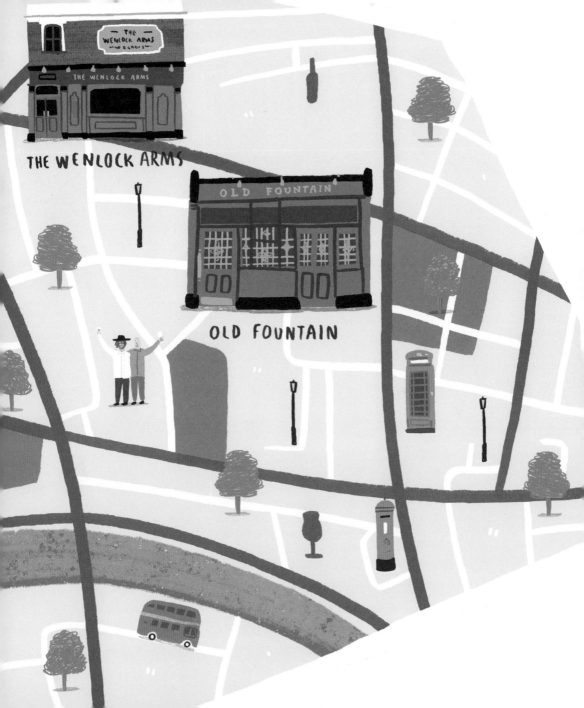

THE WENLOCK ARMS

OLD FOUNTAIN

THE HARP

HARPCOVENTGARDEN.COM

IN THE DICTIONARY UNDER 'BRITISH PUB' THERE SHOULD BE A PICTURE OF THE HARP. DRIPPING WITH HISTORY AND CENTURIES OF SPILT BEER, IT HAS MORE CHARACTER THAN ANY OTHER PUB IN LONDON, AS WELL AS THE BEST PINT OF HARVEY'S.

Usually you see the crowds before you see the pub. Seemingly squeezed until it was ten times as high as it was wide, The Harp is hard to spot but the hundreds of beer lovers aren't. On a warm night they spill out the front and across the road, round the side and up the passageway, filling the veins of cobbled streets behind. Having a sensational collection of real ales while being within drunken rolling distance of Trafalgar Square means you're bound to be busy in the evenings. But it's not the summer nights when The Harp is at its best, it's the winter afternoons – when the low sun pours through the stained-glass windows and catches the bar taps, and every blast of cold air from an opened door reminds you there's no place you'd rather be.

Called the Welsh Harp until an Irish landlady decided that couldn't stand, the pub is rich with history and character, but most of it revolves around the beer. The badge from every barrel that has ever been served in the pub is attached to the walls, making for a collage that gets more interesting the closer you get. Every surface is coated with beer antiquity, from old Crouch Vale bitters to BrewDog cask badges – BrewDog don't even make cask beer anymore. The breweries, branding and styles trace the lineage of British beer through the ages. You can read your way through the decline of mild and the rise of IPA. You can see how beer clips moved away from images of people and places into abstract design and evocative names. It is a map of where British beer

 BEERS TEN FANTASTIC REAL ALES, ONE KERNEL TAP, AND A FEW KEGS WE WON'T TALK ABOUT.

 CULTURE DURING THE DAY AN OASIS OF CALM IN THE HECTIC WEST END, BUT BY NIGHT A BUSTLING AND EXCITING PLACE TO BE, ESPECIALLY IN WINTER.

has been and where it is going, and The Harp has been there through the lot.

So have the locals. During the afternoons the pub is full of the older, newspaper-reading types who I certainly aspire to rank among in my later years. Locals are the lifeblood of this pub, although the suits and beer lovers are very welcome too. There's no doubt the pub has had to deal with a rapidly changing kind of customer and despite its slightly fusty appearance, it's a very diverse place.

The pub is now owned by Fuller's. The sale was originally greeted with concern by cask beer lovers, who assumed it would be turned into another identikit chain pub. True to their word though, the brewery have let it remain free of tie, leaving it to buy beer from the country's best traditional brewers. With the high turnover of beer you can always rely on a brewery-fresh Harvey's Bitter or, for the hopheads, something a little more modern from Dark Star. For as long as I can remember there has also been a Kernel tap, making it probably the best craft beer bar in Covent Garden in just one keg line.

If downstairs is busy (and it usually is) you can venture up the rickety staircase to a second room, which feels more like a lounge from a Sherlock Holmes novel than a pub, but it's a comfortable place to nurse a few beers and escape the madness of tourist land. All great pubs make you forget that the rest of the world is out there. For one pint or five, the people and the place are your world, and few pubs do that as well as The Harp. It is a bubble of calm at the centre of one of the world's busiest cities.

THE WENLOCK ARMS

WENLOCKARMS.COM

**TUCKED AWAY AROUND THE BACK OF CITY ROAD, THIS FORMER
WENLOCK BREWERY TAP HAS NEARLY BEEN DEMOLISHED MANY
TIMES. STILL IT STANDS, DEFIANTLY SERVING BRILLIANT CASK ALE
AND KEEPING TRADITIONS SUCH AS SAUSAGE SUNDAY ALIVE.**

For all the excitement of the craft brewing revolution, the great British pub is still declining. Closures peaked at more than fifty a week in 2009, and countless historic places are still under threat.

In 2011 a developer submitted an application to purchase and knock down The Wenlock Arms and build luxury apartments overlooking the park. The pub had been a local institution for over 150 years, pouring its first pint in 1836 as the taproom for Wenlock Brewery. Despite its rundown appearance it still served some of the most vibrant, well-kept real ales in London. The outcry was immediate and sustained, and Hackney Council rejected the proposals. Even so, the pub was under threat and the campaign continued until the unusually sympathetic council extended the canal conservation area to include the pub.

The developers didn't give up, so now the low-rise pub finds itself dwarfed by high-rise glass buildings. Thankfully, it still faces the park and there is no

way that will change. With its future assured, The Wenlock embarked on a much-needed facelift. Far from modernising, they painted the pub in its original brewery colours, removed the deathly toilets and even unearthed an original floor mosaic bearing the pub's name. The spit and sawdust décor was maintained, as was the pub's reputation for serving first-class real ale. The thankful regulars remained too, including those old enough to remember the Wenlock Brewery, which was bought out in the fifties and closed by 1962.

The only new addition to the pub was a set of ten keg taps, subtly planted into the back bar so only those with a keen eye spot them. While the hand pumps focus on traditional British bitters, pale ales and porters, the kegs are loaded with IPAs, craft lagers and even sours from London's best microbreweries. There is always something from Beavertown and Camden, but otherwise they change with the days, weeks and seasons. The food, however, never changes. Go in on a Sunday and

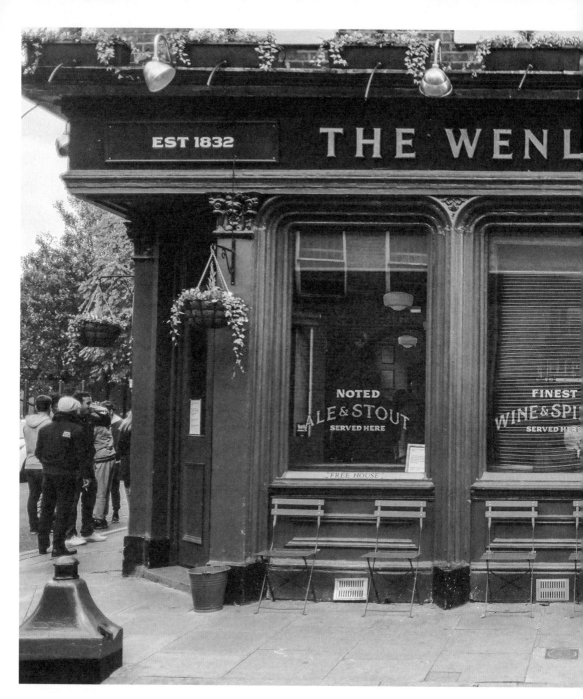

you'll benefit from Sausage Sunday, when the landlord walks around with a plate of burning hot sausages on cocktail sticks, serving them with the quiet pride a French waiter might his caviar hors d'oeuvres. The rest of the week a stained Breville sits in the corner of the bar, churning out old-school toasties for the inebriated and those whose darts game is raging out of control. It never sounds appealing until you are three pints in, and then it's all you can think about.

If the real ale brings you to The Wenlock, it's the atmosphere that makes you stay. It has a Wild West saloon vibe to it, with the wooden floors, rickety furniture and endlessly sociable locals. Some stand by the bar and help you choose a beer, some sit by the fire and occasionally remark on something they read in the paper, others just welcome a chat about the weather. Our favourite local, though, is Steve the Drummer, whose stories of being a rock star on the road and working with Motorhead's Lemmy are so wild they have to be true.

It all feels scripted somehow, but it is gloriously unplanned. The band that plays on occasional Saturdays still takes up most of the pub and is way too loud; you have to enter straight through the flight path to the dartboard, making arriving and leaving a matter of life and death; and the sloping floor makes you feel drunk as soon as you stand up.

The loss of The Wenlock could have just been another chapter in the quiet decline of the British pub. Instead it is a bastion of good beer and historic drinking culture, thankfully assured for generations to come.

BEERS	TEN BEAUTIFULLY KEPT BUT CONSERVATIVE REAL ALE PUMPS AND TEN MORE EXCITING LOCAL KEG LINES. THERE IS ALWAYS SOMETHING NEW TO TRY, ESPECIALLY IF YOU LIKE HOPS.
CULTURE	EVERYTHING A BRITISH PUB SHOULD BE – GREAT BEER, FRIENDLY LOCALS, RAUCOUS BAND NIGHTS AND QUIET SUNDAYS.

LOWLANDER GRAND CAFE

LOWLANDER.COM

THE BEST BELGIAN BEER CAFÉ IN LONDON, LOWLANDER DOESN'T GET THE LOVE IT DESERVES, PERHAPS BECAUSE NO ONE KNOWS TO ASK WHAT'S IN THE CELLAR. ONCE YOU'VE SEEN THAT LIST, YOU'LL BE BACK EVERY TIME YOU'RE IN COVENT GARDEN.

It's difficult to describe how good Belgian café culture is; the magic of being sat in some beautiful, ancient square drinking the world's best beers in the warm continental sunshine. Inside, tapsters are using the right glass to pour the right liquid at the right speed and temperature, before deftly slicing any extra head off the rim with a bar blade. In fact, it's so good it has been added to the UNESCO World Heritage list, preserved down the ages because of its importance to local culture.

It's this beautiful scene that the Lowlander Grand Cafe on Drury Lane aims to re-create. It's table service only, so the bar is lined with taps and trays that are quickly loaded with chalices of Belgian beer. The waiters carry them at head height, swerving smoothly between tables and the strewn corpses of those who have forgotten how strong Belgian beer can be. Every now and then one goes past with a steaming black bowl and you're treated to the smells of freshly cooked mussels and cream. As landlord Rich Morton says: 'Lowlander

was based on the Mort Subite bar in Brussels, and it's just evolved. The beer, the knowledge, the classic feel of that bar with table service and waiters in aprons – it was very old school there but unlike anything in London.'

So all you have to do is take your seat, pretend it's Belgium out the window (rather than an Itsu store) and feast your eyes on the beer menu. It can take a while because it is more like a bible than a menu, with well over 100 different draught and bottled beers, mostly with descriptors of their aroma and flavour. The classic Belgian beers are all there – Trappists such as Rochefort, Orval, and even Westmalle on tap – but also a selection of more unusual finds such as the brilliant, quixotic De Dolle. This fantastic Belgian brewery is run by Kris Herteleer, an eccentric artist who claims to only brew once a month (always a Saturday), but happens to make the best Belgian strong ale in the world.

The really special stuff at Lowlander never makes it on to the menu, though. Bought in tiny quantities and

239

never advertised for fear of a riot, Rich brings in some of the rarest and most exciting beers of any bar in London. He'll usually have some aged magnums of Chimay Blue in his cellar, and quite often something seasonal from Cantillon or Tilquin. Both these lambic breweries make beers that could fetch a hundred pounds on the grey market, but for Rich he just likes to know it's there so when a like-minded beer lover comes in he can show them something special. It is a unique quirk of brewers and beer lovers that they tend not to shout about the rarest, most valuable things they make or own.

Some people write off Lowlander as a tourist trap, there to service those enjoying a show at the West End or the ballet around the corner. It's true they survive on this trade, but there is a lot more to the pub and perhaps that's why I love it so much. Hiding in plain sight in the heart of the West End, if you love Belgian beer Lowlander is the only place to drink in London.

CENTRAL LONDON • Lowlander Grand Cafe

'We get a lot of Belgians and Dutch in and they love it. The most common feedback is that we have better beer than many bars in Belgium. They feel at home, and it's nice to hear. We've kept the quality of the beer and the experience.'

Lowlander is as close as we can come to the wonder that is Belgian café culture. It may lack the beautiful square and continental sunshine, but the beers are second to none, even in this amazing brewing city.

BEERS	QUIET AND CAFÉ-LIKE MOST OF THE TIME, BUT THURSDAY TO SATURDAY IT'S A HUSTLING, BUSTLING BAR THAT MAKES THE TABLE SERVICE EVEN MORE WELCOME – THE WAITERS CAN FIGHT THROUGH THE CROWDS INSTEAD OF YOU.
CULTURE	SIMPLY THE BEST BELGIAN BEER LIST IN LONDON, AND MAYBE THE UK. THERE ARE TEN TAPS AND WELL OVER 100 DIFFERENT BOTTLES IN THE FRIDGE AND CELLAR.

OLD FOUNTAIN

WHAT COULD HAVE SO EASILY BEEN A SOULLESS SILICON
ROUNDABOUT BAR HAS STUCK TO ITS GUNS, SERVING SENSATIONAL
BEER AND DELICIOUS RUSTIC PUB GRUB – ENJOYING BOTH ON
THE HIDDEN ROOF TERRACE IS ONE OF LONDON'S GREAT JOYS.

'Hidden gem' is a horribly overused phrase, but there was once no other way to describe my favourite pub in London. Tucked behind a Barclays and doing its best to look like a tired city boozer, the Old Fountain is the kind of pub you wouldn't look twice at on a night out.

Now, thanks to the complete redevelopment of The Bower nearby, the Old Fountain sits at the head of the table as you walk up from Old Street, its beige façade framed by the ultra-modern buildings around it.

Inside it is still the same old pub though – slightly dingy with rickety pub tables, brewery memorabilia on the walls and, inexplicably, a giant fish tank. As a haven from the madness of the Silicon roundabout it can't be beaten.

On tap there is always something from The Kernel and often plenty of other exciting London breweries like Beavertown, Pressure Drop and Brew By Numbers, as well as some well-chosen Belgians. On cask there's plenty to get excited about too, especially since the beer is very well looked after. It's rare to not see Oakham Citra on, one of the UK's best hoppy pale ales. If you can see past the taps, in the fridge you'll find plenty of special beer but I rarely make it that far because the draught selection never lets me down – something unique in what is essentially an extension of the City.

 BEERS — EIGHT CASK, FOURTEEN KEG AND A DECENT FRIDGE THAT'S MOSTLY FOCUSED ON BRITISH CRAFT.

 CULTURE — QUIET AND LOCAL BY DAY, BUT COME LUNCHTIME AND DINNER IT'S HEAVING. YOU'LL ALWAYS FIND A SEAT EVENTUALLY THOUGH.

OLD FOUNTAIN

It hasn't always been a beer-orientated pub. In the 1960s it was a Whitbread site, mostly serving brown bitters and continental lagers. The pub actually had more of a name as a food destination thanks to Jim Durrant, now the landlord but formerly the chef. His father owned the lease, running the pub while he cooked up classic British high cuisine, with whole salmon and lobster lunches that attracted people from the banking district.

Jim inherited the lease when his father died in 1971, even buying the building in 2006 and rescuing it from the prospect of being redeveloped. The pub wasn't just his place of employment – it wasn't even just his home – it was a stand against the gentrification that was sweeping across London.

'Someone already approached me a little while ago and asked "Would you be interested in selling because I could do this and and do that." I said, "Look, I know what you can do, but I'm not bothered in the least."' Otherwise it's another pub gone, which would be a shame because it's a nice old pub and you don't get nice old pubs anymore.'

As Old Street evolves around it, the Old Fountain is stoic and unchanging. Every now and then they add some new taps, or repaint the outside, but it always feels the same. When I started drinking there in 2010, the corner of the bar was given over to a round-faced lady in a pinny, who served up homecooked classics like shepherd's pie. Eating it from a chipped ovenproof dish, bathed in the light from the old stained windows, it was like being transported back to the 1980s. I half expected Anthony Stewart Head to bring the coffee for afters.

One day, to my horror, a sign went up saying that there would be no food served for weeks while they revamped the kitchen. When the trolley warmer went so did my favourite home chef, along with her Harvester-sized portions of lasagne and chips. Much as I miss them, the new chefs have more than made up for it with their seasonal selection of salads, burgers and roasts. Because the kitchen is open you can see them toiling away, and witness the passion and fresh ingredients that go into every dish. The halloumi salad is delicious and the chips are some of the best in London, cooked golden, crispy and wickedly just a little bit oily. A bowl of these and a pint of Kernel pale ale on their well-hidden roof terrace is all you really need from life.

THE EXMOUTH ARMS

EXMOUTHARMS.COM

FOUND ON ONE OF THE BEST FOODIE STREETS IN LONDON, THE EXMOUTH ARMS MAKES SURE THE BEER QUALITY KEEPS UP WITH THE CUISINE WITH A HUGE TAP AND BOTTLE LIST.

Exmouth Market is London in miniature. It has grand buildings, old-fashioned lampposts and cobbles. Boutique clothing stores bump up against cornershops, a food market trades outside a world-class restaurant, and a terrible pub is made up for by a sensational one further down the street. The Exmouth Arms at the west end of the street doesn't look like much from the outside but there is always that festive kind of buzz coming out of the doors. Sat on the corner, it sends the sound of clinking glasses, laughter and chatter in three directions, drawing you in with warmth. Most pubs around Clerkenwell are empty at the weekends as the new media and PR types head out of London for the weekend, but The Exmouth Arms chatters all week long. Sometimes the atmosphere is so party-like you wonder whether you've accidentally crashed a work do.

You can see the pub has a story to tell, with some original décor from when it was undoubtedly a less than respectable boozer. With stained-glass or rippled windows, it's slightly dingy even in summer; but it's

the beer that brings people in. Good stuff is hard to find around these parts so The Exmouth Arms has all tastes covered and then some. It's part of the Barworks chain of pubs and bars that takes its drinks very seriously. If you walk into a bar in a prime location with amazing beer, it's very likely it's a Barworks. Among them are The Black Heart in Camden, the Well and Bucket in Shoreditch and The Kings Arms of Bethnal Green. They don't feel like a chain though, being unique in their vibe, look and beer lists.

Starting out with the entire Camden core range, The Exmouth Arms gives itself the freedom to serve whatever it damn well pleases on its fourteen keg lines and four cask handpulls. There's no seasonal approach or balance of light and dark, they simply buy the best thing available at the time, which can make for a very eclectic mix. You'll always find something delicious from London, but a whole load of Manchester and West Country beer too, as well as imports from around the world. They're huge fans of Scandi beer, which means

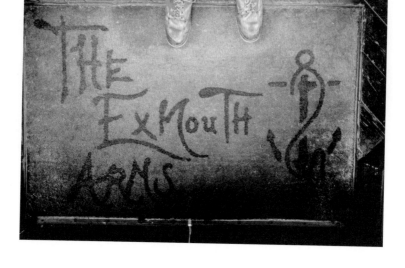

Lervig and To Øl make regular appearances and light up the bar with their more experimental approach to brewing hop-forward beers. Whenever it's available you'll see Lervig and Magic Rock's collaboration, Farmhouse IPA, a funky, sherberty take on an IPA that never ceases to amaze me.

The real fun is in the fridges though, where the high turnover from the busy bar means they can be pretty daring in what they bring in. As well as a couple of Belgian beauties, you'll find Cascade Brewing, a sour brewery flown in all the way from Oregon, and many other lovely things from Stateside. Some of the sharing bottles will cost you over £20, but the chance to try these ultra-rare beers shouldn't be sniffed at. While hoppy beers need to be drunk fresh (making local IPAs preferable), sour beers can benefit from a bit of time in bottle and might even taste better for the journey across the Atlantic.

Along with the food market, The Exmouth Arms has helped make Exmouth Market an unlikely destination just outside of the Square Mile. It's now the kind of place you could get some world-class beer and food within ten steps – and that rubbish bar I mentioned earlier happens to have table football and a late licence, so there's really no need to leave the market at all.

 BEERS — FOURTEEN LINES OF ECLECTIC AMERICAN, BELGIAN, SCANDI AND BRITISH BEER. FOUR CASK HANDPULLS BUT NOTHING WILL REALLY STAND OUT UNLESS THERE IS AN EVENT ON.

 CULTURE — BUSY CITY PUB (ESPECIALLY FROM 5 UNTIL 7) BUT A VERY FRIENDLY CLIENTELE IS USUALLY THERE BEFORE THEY HEAD HOME OR TO MORRO, THE INCREDIBLE TAPAS RESTAURANT OVER THE ROAD.

THE EXMOUTH ARMS

CRAFT BEERS & SPIRITS
FROM AROUND THE WORLD

HOME COOKED FOOD

5cc COCKTAILS UPSTAIRS
FROM 6PM
(TUE - SAT)

Nº 23

CHOOSING A LONDON PUB

THERE ARE WELL OVER 5,000 PUBS IN LONDON AND NEARLY 100 BREWERIES. AS YOU READ THIS SOME PASSIONATE BEER LOVER IS PREPARING TO OPEN ANOTHER AND, FOR EVERY ONE OF THEM, THERE ARE TEN MORE DREAMING OF IT.

—

It was inevitable we would leave some out, and that some would open while this book was printed. This is only one fleeting moment in a timeline that dates back centuries and will go on for many more. Things will change, but these stories of how we got here will give you the knowledge to drink better beers in the right places. Between the lines are lessons on spotting pubs that buy quality beer, look after it and serve it fresh. It teaches you to look for blackboards and paper menus as proof of changing, seasonal produce. Hopefully it has encouraged you to never buy a beer without trying it first, and not to be misled by claims of 'a beer garden out back' anywhere in Zone 1.

My favourite lesson though, one that I learnt while researching this book, is the best time to go to the pub. For me, it is Saturday lunchtime, early enough to get the best seat and watch as the sun seeps through the windows and people pour through the door. It's a peaceful time in any pub, one when you can hear friends talk and yourself think. Often I reflect on the fact that there is no better place in the world to drink beer than London. Its history and its people are written on the walls of boozers from Hillingdon right out to the Isle of Dogs. From the green tiles of former Truman's pubs to the trendiest 30-tap bars of Shoreditch, they cater to everyone. In researching this book I've watched drag queens bring East End dives to life, and ageing regulars in renovated gastropubs telling the same stories they've told at the bar for 50 years.

The pub is both the refuge and the adventure in our daily lives. It is the place we meet our best friends and find new ones. From the ill-advised Monday night out to the well-earned Friday pint, we gravitate towards it in search of something better than the drudgery of the day. Even in the height of winter, when London is grey and sketched in concrete, the breadth and colour of London's pubs is a marvel.

There are just as many miracles in our breweries, whose products fill the veins of the pubs and give them life. While they look broadly the same, that only points out two important truths: that it's the tiny idiosyncrasies that make them special, and that

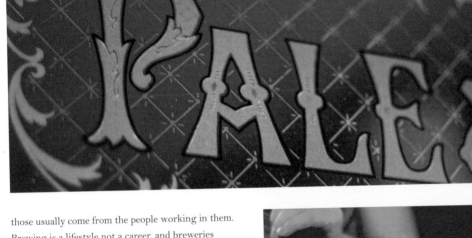

those usually come from the people working in them. Brewing is a lifestyle not a career, and breweries become extensions of the people who own them. The Kernel is modest, quiet but bustling; Weird Beard is scuzzy and exciting; Brew By Numbers full of quirks and playfulness; Camden full of steely ambition. The personality of each one comes through in its beers to make this brewing scene perhaps the most diverse in the world. You can see heavy influences right from the West Coast of America, through Burton-on-Trent to Flanders, Bavaria, Berlin and Pilsen – sometimes all within one brewery.

London has finally returned to its beery glory days. Companies that started in damp corners of pub cellars or garages will soon be household names, pouring beers across the country and around the globe. We are a brewing nation again and our capital is leading the way through multiculturalism and a spirit of adventure.

There has never been a better time to be a drink beer, and there has never been a better place to be a beer drinker than in London.

INDEX

ACKNOWLEDGEMENTS

JONNY WOULD LIKE TO THANK:

Brad first and foremost, for the books and the memories. He'd also like to thank his beautiful Heather whose patience and kindness makes so many things possible. Finally, huge cheers to all the people in this book, without whom there would have been nothing to write about.

BRAD WOULD LIKE TO THANK:

Jonny – the endlessly talented, incredibly generous and dependably drunk man that I've had the great fortune of sharing this crazy and exciting journey with. Here's to many more.

I'd also like to extend big love to all my friends and family who have helped me through a tough couple of years – especially my mother George, who's been my rock, my sister Georgina and brother-in-law Steve. And lastly my father Terry, who was the coolest guy I have ever met and one of my best friends. I miss him greatly every day.